HOW TO INSTALL
CERAMIC TILE

*Created and designed by
the editorial staff of
ORTHO BOOKS*

Project Director
Karin Shakery

Writers
Jill Fox
and the Editors of
Ortho Books

Illustrators
Ron Hildebrand
Richard Moore

Photographer
Joyce OudkerkPool

Ortho Books

Publisher
Edward A. Evans

Editorial Director
Christine Robertson

Production Director
Ernie S. Tasaki

Managing Editors
Michael D. Smith
Sally W. Smith

System Manager
Katherine L. Parker

Address all inquiries to:
Ortho Books
Box 5006
San Ramon, CA 94583-0906

Copyright © 1989
Monsanto Company
All rights reserved under international and
Pan-American copyright conventions.

11	12	13	14
97	98	99	00

ISBN 0-89721-142-1
Library of Congress Catalog Card
Number 87-72099

THE SOLARIS GROUP
2527 Camino Ramon
San Ramon, CA 94583

Consultants & Contributors

Adamson House
Malibu Lagoon State Beach
Malibu, Calif.
Phyllis Perskie
Burson-Marsteller Public Relations
New York, N.Y.
Diana von Welczeck
Dillon Tile Supply
San Francisco, Calif.
Joseph Feuling
San Francisco, Calif.
Robert Hund
Marble Institute of America
Farmington, Mich.
Harvey Powell
Materials & Methods Standards
Association
Grand Haven, Mich.
Nicholas Loomis
Pittsburg Corning Corp
Pittsburg, Penn.
David Cardwell
Pittsburg Corning Corp
San Jose, Calif.
Dan Simoni, CSI
Quamagra Tile
San Francisco, Calif.
Tile Council of America
Princeton, N.J.

Designers, Installers & Manufacturers

Ace Architects
Oakland, Calif.
Pages 33, 45
Tina Ayers
Oakland, Calif.
Front cover, pages 9, 13, 17, 21, 23, 34, 69, 71
Kelley Hale
Hale Remodeling, Inc.
El Cerrito, Calif.
Pages 15, 30, 59
Heath Ceramics, Inc.
Sausalito, Calif.
Pages 10 (top), 17, 74
Steve Hedden
Hercules, Calif.
Pages 15, 30, 59
James Henrietta
Building and Remodel Associates
San Francisco, Calif.
Page 82 (top)

Ron Hinrich
R & R Craftmasters
San Mateo, Calif.
Pages 51, 88
McIntyre Tile Company
Healdsburg, Calif.
Page 23
Sten Volpe for
Michael Taylor Designs, Inc.
San Francisco, Calif.
Page 35
Jan Newman
Burlingame, Calif.
Pages 51, 88
Larry Parker
Orinda, Calif.
Page 71
Dan Phipps & Associates
San Francisco, Calif.
Pages 7, 81, 82 (bottom)
Steve Rockstroh
Corrales, N.M.
Pages 13, 23, 71
Roger Chetrit
Tile Visions
San Francisco, Calif.
Pages 10 (bottom), 51, 57, 72, 88

Front cover: Tiled surfaces do not have to be rigid grids. Once you've mastered the basic tile-setting techniques, try being a little more adventurous and design installations such as this circular one.

Page 1: This garden wall is covered in Moorish-influenced tiles that were produced in the 1920s by Malibu Potteries. They still look as attractive and colorful as they did when originally installed.

Back cover

Upper left: Diagonal corners on large floor tiles allow for dropping in a small square in a contrasting color.

Upper right: Rectangular tiles are installed in a vertical pattern in this glass-enclosed shower. A tiled bath surround extends into the shower area providing a bench on which to sit or place supplies.

Lower left: Tiles can be installed on a variety of surfaces. At the Adamson House in Malibu, different shapes and textures are used to create a singular patio.

Lower right: A tiled staircase is long-lasting and easy to clean. However, care should be taken when using hand-made pavers. This sort of tile has uneven surfaces and individual tiles often vary slightly in size and dimension.

HOW TO INSTALL
CERAMIC TILE

Designing with Tile

Materials

Installing Tile

Care & Repair

DESIGNING WITH TILE

Colorful, versatile, durable ceramic tile has been used as a decorating element for hundreds of years. Yet it is still as up-to-date as any product invented in the twentieth century.

Featured throughout these pages are installations to inspire you and excite you about the possibilities of introducing tile into your home. As well as ceramic and mosaic tile, you will see marble, slate, and granite products.

Installing tile is a project that many people assume should be left to professionals. However, the only tricky part is the layout. Once you have ascertained where the first tile goes you are on your way. The rest of the work is messy and time-consuming—but very rewarding.

Inspiration for decorating ideas can be found in books, magazines, and showrooms. Also look for interesting ideas in the buildings you work, shop, and bank in.

THE BENEFITS OF TILE

Ceramic tile is basically a slab of kiln-fired clay. This humble definition belies a product that is as good-looking as it is practical. A lot of people have already discovered its merits and the use of tile in the home has doubled in the last ten years. Ceramic tile is tough, easy to clean, and fireproof. Tiles are also dazzlingly colorful and durable—some installations are older than written history.

The ease of installation makes tile a good choice for the do-it-yourselfer looking for a creative and rewarding project. And the ease of maintenance makes tile a perfect choice for those with a busy life-style.

Versatility

Tile can be installed on horizontal and vertical surfaces, indoors and out, and used where it will be exposed to water or to high heat.

Ceramic tiles and related products can decorate virtually every room of the house. Although it is most often seen in kitchens and bathrooms, tile can be used as a practical floor covering in an entry way or family room, a colorful accent on stair risers, an easy-to-clean surface on a coffee table, and a practical and good-looking fireplace surround and hearth.

Tile is an efficient solar energy collector and, installed on the floor of a sunroom or greenhouse, will retain and radiate heat.

Outside, tile can be used to pave a patio, cover steps and risers, or to decorate a fountain or a low wall.

Exciting ideas and creative uses of ceramic tile and pavers are shown throughout this chapter. Because they are installed in the same manner as ceramic tile, this book also features marble, slate, and granite tile. These products are collectively referred to as dimensioned stone.

Variety

The variety of tile colors, shapes, and sizes currently on the market presents a creative challenge to designers—both professional and amateur.

You can find glazed ceramic tiles in a rainbow of fashion colors. Hues range from quiet neutrals to blazing primaries, from pretty pastels to dramatic dark colors. Unglazed tiles, once featured only in terra-cotta, now come in a full range of earth tones, from palest sand to darkest brown.

There are tiles with dainty floral decorations, crisp stripes, delft motifs, and numerous other designs. Some tiles are handmade with uneven edges and surface variations. Others are mass produced to look as if they were handcrafted. Many tiles are textured, both for better grip underfoot and for an interesting look.

There is an infinite variety of sizes and shapes readily available. Sizes range from 1- to 12- inch squares; shapes include rectangles, hexagons, circles, and octagons.

It is not difficult to give an installation a professional finish. Many manufacturers offer a large selection of trim and corner pieces. These trim tiles enable you to turn a corner neatly, ring a recessed washbasin, cap a splashback, and edge a counter or table. If the particular tile you have chosen does not include trim pieces, select trim from another

range or manufacturer. You can mix and match at will as long as trim tiles are the same thickness and work with your colors and your design.

Many tile manufacturers also produce matching accessories, including towel bars, soap dishes, cookbook holders, and spice racks.

This wide variety of products provides a virtually endless palette of possibilities. Many of these are defined and described in chapter two.

Easy Installation

Any reasonably handy do-it-yourselfer can install ceramic tile and related products using the installation techniques that are presented in chapter three.

Traditionally, tile was installed using a mortar bed, a tricky procedure. Although some installations—namely swimming pools, uneven floors, and curved walls—are best left to professionals, most ceramic tile jobs can be installed using the simple thinsetting techniques outlined in chapter three.

New products, including premixed organic mastics, premixed grouts, latex caulk, and plastic spacers, also help to simplify the installation process. These products are described in chapter two.

Improvements in the manufacturing of marble, slate, and granite tiles make them as easy to install as ceramic tile.

New setting and spacing products have revolutionized the installation of glass blocks, which can now be installed in a manner very similar to that of ceramic and dimensioned stone tiles. For this reason, glass block installation is presented on page 80.

New materials and simple installation methods (see page 80) have made glass block very popular, especially for use in bathrooms. The grid patterns they form integrate well with ceramic tile.

Easy Maintenance

Ceramic and stone tiled walls, floors, and countertops are easy to care for. Tile floors should be swept or vacuumed regularly to remove gritty particles that might scratch them. Routine cleaning consists of a quick wipe with a damp mop or a sponge. Even when neglected for a long time, a good wash will usually bring back the lustrous sheen.

In chapter four you will find tips on removing stains, methods for solving special problems, and specific maintenance guidelines to keep your tile looking new for years to come.

Durability

As long as the original installation was properly done and as long as you do not get bored with the color or design, there is no reason why a tiled floor, wall, or counter should not last as long as your house. (When the burial tomb of the Pharaoh Zoser was opened in 1803, the blue-green glazed tiles inside were as beautiful as if they had been recently installed. In fact, the Stepped Pyramid in the Nile Valley was built about 4700 BC.)

When selecting tile, bear in mind that you will be living with it for a very long time. Choose colors and plan designs that you think will still be appropriate when it comes time to replace the furnishings.

Easy Replacement

If wall-to-wall carpeting gets stained or burned, you usually have to replace the entire piece. However, if damage occurs to a tiled floor, individual tiles can be replaced without tearing out the entire installation.

Cracked or loose tiles and damaged grout can easily be repaired and rejuvenated using the methods described in chapter four.

If you want to make changes for purely aesthetic reasons, most tile installations can be restyled, accented, or added to without having to remove the main body of the existing tile.

It is also possible to extend a tile installation should you decide to enlarge or add on to a room. Even if you cannot match the existing tile at the time of remodeling, you can install a border pattern and continue tiling into the new area. Or you can remove a few of the existing tiles and spot in accent tiles that match the new installation thereby tying the two areas together visually.

Solar Benefits

Ceramic tile is an efficient solar collector, and one of the best floor coverings to install for that purpose. In the winter, tile stores heat during the day and slowly releases it at night. In the summer, tile defuses some of the sun's rays by absorbing heat. Then in the evening, ventilation carries the heat away.

Consider installing tiles around wall heaters and radiators, around wood stoves, and under skylights to achieve the greatest benefits.

If you are installing tile primarily for solar heat benefits, the best substrate is a thick bed of concrete. However, even installed over plywood, tiles will store and emit heat to some extent.

Important Properties

The important properties to look for when selecting ceramic tile are solar absorbance, conductivity and thermal diffusiveness, and heat emission.

Absorbance evaluates the amount of heat the tile will absorb. The higher the number the better for this purpose. Darker-colored tiles tend to have higher solar absorbance.

Conductivity and thermal diffusiveness measure the speed at which the heat passes through the tile and can be stored in the backing material. A high number is best.

Heat emission refers to the ability of the tile to radiate the stored heat out into the room. This is very important if you want to use the tile as a nighttime heat source in winter. Many tiles will absorb and store heat, but not all will emit it well.

Value

Ceramic tile looks so good that many people consider it a luxury product. Actually, it is very affordable. Many ceramic floor tiles are about the same price as vinyl flooring. In addition, tile will long outlast vinyl installations, so in the long run it is much more economical.

A tiled countertop will cost more than plastic laminate but less than a stone or simulated stone slab.

Tiling a wall is more expensive than either painting or hanging wallcovering. But because of their water resistance, tiles are more practical in many locations.

An important consideration when weighing the benefits of tile against other products is the return for your money. Floors, walls, and counters covered with ceramic tile, marble, slate, and related products are generally associated with luxury living. Therefore an installation that looks professional will almost certainly add to both the appeal and value of your house should you decide to sell it.

A clever combination of colors and sizes makes a strong statement in keeping with the unusual placement of the fireplace. (It is raised so that it can be clearly viewed from the bed.) However, an installation of this kind requires careful planning.

Above: You can install colored tiles in a definite pattern or place them randomly. Here, an abstract design mimics the colors of the spectacular vista enjoyed from this patio.

Right: It is not necessary to sink the tub in order to create a sense of luxury. Tiled steps enclose a tub and form a wall-to-wall raised platform.

DESIGNING WITH TILE

Designing a tile installation is not mysterious or difficult but it does require some time and effort. You need to understand certain principles of design and some requirements that are unique to the product. Remember, too, that your tile installation must be coordinated with all the other elements of the room.

Principles of Design

The goal of design is to find a balance between functional needs and aesthetic pleasure. This idea, common to all design processes, is referred to as appropriate fit.

Think of fit as picking out a shirt to wear. Obviously, the selection process goes beyond choosing an item that is the right size. It includes judging whether it is flattering, whether it is suitable for the occasion (or your mood), and whether it coordinates with other items in your wardrobe. Selecting an appropriate piece of clothing comes naturally after a few years of choosing what to wear every day, but understanding how to apply the same criteria to a tile installation may take a little effort. The following contains some basic rules on form, scale, rhythm, and axis.

Form

The principle of form relates to the shape and structure of the various elements in a design. Forms should balance and complement one an-

other. Too many curves, angles, and rectangles within a small space will make an uncomfortable design.

Circular forms give a feeling of closure that can be comforting. Use curves in areas that you want to look distinct—for example, a patio that you consider an outdoor room or a shower area within a large bathroom.

Scale

Scale is an expression of relative size. The principle of scale refers to the relationship between different elements within a room. Scale in the tile design would affect the size of the individual tiles, the proportion of different tiled areas to each other, and items such as the height of the tub surround as compared to the ceiling height.

Rhythm

Like the ordered flow of rhythm in music, the principle of rhythm in design involves the ordered regularity of the elements in the room. The use of similar forms in the same scale will create a constant beat, so to speak, uniting the design. The steady grid of square tiles paired with other square elements, for instance a wall of glass blocks, forms this kind of clear connection. Repeating colors and using the same color scheme in several rooms of the house is another way to achieve a cohesive look.

Axis

The principle of axis is a visual orientation that relates to the way in which objects in a setting attract your eye, causing you to focus on them. The axis of a room is determined by your line of sight as you view focal points. You can form an axis with tile by the way you set up the grid, forcing the eye in one direction or another. Adding a stripe of tile of contrasting color or texture is another way to form axis. Axis lines should align with doorways, windows, the fireplace mantel, or follow the curve of a hallway or the rise of the stairs.

Color

People are affected by color both consciously and subconsciously. You feel as well as see color. Experiments have shown that color affects blood pressure, pulse, metabolic rates, brain activity, and biorhythms. Because color sets a mood, color selection is very important to the impact a room will have on the activities that take place within it.

While you might be choosing a particular color tile to mix well with other elements of the decor, you should consider some of these larger issues. Remember, the tile will last a very long time and impact your home for years.

Using all one color—a monochromatic scheme—can have a quieting effect. It can also become boring. Using multiple colors in a polychromatic design can be exciting, but if overdone can be exhausting and create a look that you may tire of quickly. The number of colors you can put together effectively in your tile work is also dependent on the other elements in the room: the furniture and the accessories. To put together a unified design you must also keep in mind the colors of these elements

One way to put several colors together successfully is to copy combinations of colors that are found together naturally. Orange, purple, green, and aqua may seem like a wild combination, but these are the colors found in the Bird of Paradise, a flower that grows naturally in southern California. Look at other flowers for interesting color schemes.

If you are planning an intricate combination of colors, stripes, or patterns, first test the effect on paper.

Choosing a Color

You should be aware of color terminology if you are going to discuss color possibilities with a designer. Hue refers to a color by name—red, blue, green, mauve. Value defines the relative darkness or lightness of the hue. Colors of lower value are dark, those of higher value are pale. Chroma defines the saturation of a color. Strong chroma means a color that is rich and full. Weak chroma means a color with a flat look.

Consider these guidelines when you are deciding on a color:

☐ Ignore the name of the color; it can influence you more than you think.

☐ If you know that you want green, consider the full range of greens and think about combining different shades.

☐ Pay attention to an immediate response to a particular color. That impulse indicates your emotional preference.

☐ Narrow down your choices to three or four.

☐ Borrow or buy a few samples of each of your choices and take them home with you.

☐ Remove as many colors as possible from the room where you plan to install the tile. (Put drop cloths over surfaces that can't be removed.)

☐ Place the samples in the room in which they are to be installed. Look at the tiles in different areas of the room. The same tile may look slightly darker on the floor than on the wall. Check the color at different times of the day and under different lighting conditions. Artificial light will change the appearance. Incandescent light adds a pinkish tone. Depending on the particular tube, fluorescent light may change the hue completely.

☐ Look at the samples together with paint chips and wallcovering, carpet, and upholstery samples.

Size

The basic rule is that small tiles look good in small rooms and large tiles look better in large rooms. Small tiles tend to expand the size of the surface; large tiles to decrease it.

If you are using more than one size tile in the same room, use larger tiles on a horizontal surface rather than on a vertical one; and use larger tiles on lower surfaces rather than on higher ones. Avoid tiling a countertop with tiles that are larger than the ones on the floor—this will make the room look top-heavy. A wall covered with tiles that are larger than the ones on the floor will also look awkward.

These guidelines should be considered, but remember that installations are very individual. Use your judgement, testing the tile size in the location, as you test the color.

Shape

The majority of ceramic and dimensioned stone tiles are square. Square tiles are the most versatile, and the easiest to install. Other common shapes include hexagons, rectangles (usually about the size of a standard brick), and octagons, which are especially effective when combined with small square spots of a contrasting color.

Realize that shape can also be determined by color. By using borders, stripes, and contrasting colors, you can create dramatic shapes using square tiles.

Pattern

You can form optical illusions by laying tile in different patterns (different grids). Individual areas in one room can be defined by borders or a shift in color. Tiles set on the diagonal can appear to change the dimensions.

Colored stripes and swirls will create special effects.

Grout Joints

There are two design factors that should be considered when selecting grout: One is the color, the other is the width of the joint—the space between tiles.

Grout is available in a huge spectrum of colors (one manufacturer lists 89 shades in its catalog). Grout that contrasts with the tile will emphasize the geometry of the installation. This can be stunning if done well. However, it will also make any flaws or irregularities in width or placement much more pronounced.

To deemphasize the grid, choose grout colors that match the tiles or are so neutral as to become almost invisible. If you are installing decorative tiles, match the grout color to the background color. If you don't, the decoration will be fighting for attention with the grout.

Joint size is generally a matter of taste and style. Most important is that the joints are uniform throughout the installation. Practical considerations include the fact that wide joints tend to be weaker and may crack (a ⅛-inch-wide joint is considered narrow; ½ inch is wide). They are also somewhat more difficult to keep clean.

Lighting

As noted previously, lighting will impact the color of the tile. Tile will also impact the lighting. Track lights and ceiling-mounted fixtures will cause bright spots if they shine directly onto a tiled surface.

Having a place to sit in a shower adds to both comfort and safety. Note how the top of the bench is sloped so that water rolls off toward the drain. The owners felt no need for an enclosure, instead the designer provided them with a low wall which can be used as a hand grip when climbing over the high curb.

TILE AROUND THE HOUSE

W hatever the size or the style of a house, there is a surface that will benefit by finishing it with ceramic tile, dimensioned stone, or glass block. Let your imagination run wild. If the results are more extravagant than your budget can bear, begin with a few simple projects.

Above: *Don't overlook possibilities for adding color and pattern to the exterior of your home. Colorful tiles can hide ugly foundations and wrap around window ledges.*
Left: *Many individual tiles are designed to form larger patterns when combined. These patterns form permanent, practical art. The addition of tile around the mailboxes of this apartment building makes the area attractive and easy to maintain.*

Angles of the hearth are underlined by changing direction when installing unglazed pavers on the floor, the area around the fireplace, and the window seat. (Be sure to have throw pillows or a rug on hand to soften and warm this hard seating.)

Entrance Halls

First impressions are important: Entrances should be inviting and introduce your decorating style.

Whether your entrance is a distinct hallway or merely part of the living room, it can be defined by the strong grid pattern of a tile installation.

The total floor area is usually small enough to allow you to splurge on materials. Choose glazed or unglazed tiles that are not slippery when wet.

Stairs

Steps and stairs are one of the most dramatic elements in your home and their role in your design scheme should not be overlooked.

When choosing materials it is important to take safety into account. For treads, select sturdy floor tiles with a textured surface for slip resistance. Use trim pieces on the edges or trim edges with wood. By accenting risers you'll also make the stairs safer by clearly pointing out each step. Install tiles across the full width of the riser or set individual tiles as a riser accent.

Kitchens

A kitchen is the heart of a home, the center of family activities, and the gathering place at parties; this room provides tremendous opportunities for creative use of tile.

Materials installed in kitchens must resist water, steam, grease, and odors, and should be easy to clean. Ceramic tile fulfills all of these requirements.

Although ceramic or dimensioned stone tiled floors will be long lasting and good-looking, be aware that they can be cold and hard underfoot. Rugs in front of sinks and work counters will ease the strain.

Vertical spaces behind a stove, around a wall oven, and on backsplashes provide ideal areas for the creative use of color, pattern, and design. Tile is a practical and hygienic choice for these areas as well as for work surfaces, countertops, sink surrounds, bar tops, and tables.

Bathrooms

Today's bathrooms are important centers in the home. Many combine standard needs with saunas, whirlpools, workout centers, and relaxation areas.

Surfaces in bathrooms have to withstand water, steam, moisture, and heat, and be easy to clean. Be sure to check the water absorbency of any tile destined to come in contact with water. When in doubt, use a sealer.

Around a shower or tub, use glazed floor tiles with a matte finish or a texture for slip resistance. Or use mosaics—the additional grout required by the smaller tiles will make a wet floor less slippery.

Accessory pieces such as soap dishes, towel, and paper holders are also offered. Some tile makers have keyed their tile colors to match colors of toilets, sinks, bidets, and tubs made by leading manufacturers.

Family Rooms

The social center of many homes is the family room. Some family rooms are formal areas; others are entertainment centers; still others are extensions of the kitchen.

Family room floors are the most obvious choice for tile. You'll have an easy time cleaning up messes made by pets, children, and party guests.

Other uses for tile in the family room include fireplace surrounds, hearths, countertops, bars, tabletops, and architectural accents around doors and windows.

Fireplaces

Tile is well suited to decorating many different parts of a fireplace. The hearth can be covered with ceramic tile, slate, marble, or brick that will withstand heat. A tiled mantel provides a backdrop for interesting displays. The area surrounding the opening provides ample opportunity for the creative use of tiles. And the breast (front of the chimney) can be tiled to become permanent artwork.

Doors & Windows

Ceramic tiles around doors and windows add decorative touches.

Use tiles around door frames to add color to a vertical surface. You can run tiles solidly around the opening or place individual tile accents. To emphasize an arched opening, use tiles to define the curve.

Tiles are especially effective used on deeply set windows where the ledges are used as shelves for plants or collectibles.

Ceramic tiles are both a decorative and a practical treament for a greenhouse window. They will absorb and reflect heat to the plants, and make it easy to clean up water and dirt spills.

Patios, Porches & Paths

All tiles for outdoor use should be slip resistant. If you live in an area where there is a chance of freezing, be careful to select tile products that can withstand freeze-thaw conditions.

Be sure to slope the site so that paved areas drain quickly and puddles and slippery spots don't form.

Fountains

The sight, sound, and scent of splashing water is traditional in hot climates. A tiled foundation is a way of introducing water and color into your landscape.

Architectural Tiles

Place ceramic tiles above window casings, around door frames, on roof framing, across eaves, and around dormers to add interest to the architectural lines of the building. Add tiles in a design above a garage door, on the front door, and on window boxes as spots of color to enliven an otherwise plain elevation.

Tile Siding

Tile acts as a practical siding material. It will last for generations and an occasional hosing is all that's needed for years of shining beauty.

Even if you don't tile the entire wall, consider using it on areas of the house that are often touched. For example, areas around mailboxes, door knobs, hand rails, and stairs. And, use ceramic tiles anywhere near water or moisture, such as at the bottom of drainpipes and as a backsplash for a fountain or splash box.

Signage

Number and letter tiles that form your name or address are an attractive addition to a door or mailbox.

If you designed your own home, you may want to "sign" it. Architect Frank Lloyd Wright installed a distinctive square red tile bearing his signature on every building he designed.

Three shades of handmade tile were carefully sorted then arranged into this circular pattern. The grout was blended to match.

MATERIALS

Tile installation can be thought of as a sandwich of products—layers of materials stacked one on top of the other. This chapter pulls apart the layers, outlines the ingredients, and discusses the considerations involved in making an informed selection.

The most obvious layer is, of course, the tile itself. Ceramic tile and related products such as marble, granite, and slate are defined and their uses explained.

Setting materials—the adhesives and grout—are the next layer. The best choice varies with the type of tile used and the location of the installation.

Under the adhesive is the substrate or backing. A high-quality installation requires proper backing materials.

There are many different materials and substrates on the market. Your efforts in researching the available products will be rewarded by a professional-looking and long-lasting tile installation.

SELECTING TILE

T he wide range of tile colors, shapes, and sizes that makes the design so exciting can be a bit daunting when you're standing in a tile store trying to choose the right product for your installation.

Although the look of the tile is important, its quality in relation to the type of installation it will be used for is more important. In making a choice, consider the location and type of installation and the amount of use the area will get. The following information is intended to help you choose the right tile and to make accurate estimates of the number of tiles you'll need.

Where to Buy Tile

Ceramic tile and related products are sold at home-improvement centers and tile showrooms maintained by manufacturers, distributors, and dealers. Showrooms often have displays of typical installations that can help when choosing tile patterns and designs. The showroom staff and manufacturers' literature can be important sources of ideas on designs and new products.

A local telephone directory is a good source for locating tile outlets. If there are no tile outlets near you, contact the tile manufacturers—some of them will send their product catalogs and allow you to order tile directly from them.

Types of Installations

There are several characteristics of any installation that must be considered when choosing tile. These are described below; the chart on pages 26 and 27 lists the correct types of tile and setting materials to use for various typical tile installations. Tiles are categorized according to their resistance to water, their glazes, and their textures. The correct setting materials are determined by the location and the type of tile. Each type of tile and setting material is defined elsewhere in this chapter.

Wet and Dry Installations

Location—indoors or outdoors, wet or dry—is the overriding factor in choosing the correct tile for any installation.

A wet area is defined as a surface that is either soaked, saturated, or subjected to moisture or liquid. All exterior locations are considered wet areas. Indoor wet areas include tub enclosures, showers, laundry rooms, saunas, steam rooms, swimming pools, and countertops that contain sinks. Tiles installed in wet areas must be water-resistant; the setting materials must tolerate moisture; and the substrate must be water-resistant and should be installed over a waterproof membrane.

Freezing Conditions

Exterior locations in cold climates require installing tiles with freeze-thaw stability. Tiles installed outdoors in these locations must be able to withstand significant changes in temperature without cracking.

Type of Tile Project

Whether the tile will be installed on a horizontal or vertical surface is another consideration that should be of concern. Choices of glaze, texture, and tile thickness are affected by the exact location of the tile installation: floor, wall, countertop, or other area.

Amount of Use

The amount of use a tile installation will get is another determining factor. Only you, the tile user, will know how much use the installation is likely to receive.

Similarly, all countertops are not alike. A countertop bar in the family room, used mainly as a place to set drinks, gets much less use than the countertop next to the kitchen sink. And even that kitchen countertop receives a very different type of use than the countertop in the utility room, which may be used for repotting plants and washing the dog.

Exterior Floors

When selecting tiles for exterior patio and porch installations, choose a nonslip surface. For installations that will be subjected to freezing weather, choose vitreous tiles and include appropriate additives in both the adhesive and the grout.

Quarry pavers are an excellent choice for outdoor use. They are both attractive and durable. If you plan to use stone, select honed or torched dimensioned stone, both of which are textured; polished stone can be dangerously slippery when wet or icy.

The best substrate for exterior tile is a concrete slab. The slab should be sloped so that water drains from the surface of tiles.

Consider using a penetrating sealer on the finished installation. The sealer will help prevent stains and will bring out the natural luster of pavers and stone products. When you purchase the tile, consult the salespeople for recommendations on sealers.

The designer used seven different colored tiles to create this double shower/tub enclosure. The wave design has dimension as well as shape: It protrudes slightly from the tiled walls.

Plan View Drawing

A plan view drawing acts as both a design tool and the basis for estimating your tile and adhesive needs. This simple drawing is a valuable reference tool when designing the installation and when purchasing and laying out the tile. Keep a copy of it for guidance throughout the project.

Using a pencil, a straightedge, and ¼- or ⅛-inch graph paper, make a scale drawing of all surfaces to be tiled. Show all critical dimensions and features. Note the locations of sinks, fixtures, and appliances as well as drawer, cupboard, and appliance door clearances. Note where walls abut the countertop and where the countertop must be finished with trim tiles. Record dimensions of the entire area and everything in the space that will affect the tile installation.

Estimating Materials

The square footage of the area to be tiled determines the amounts of tile and setting materials required. To determine the square footage, multiply the length of the area by the width. Calculate the square footage of different parts of the area to be covered (a countertop and a backsplash, or a wall and a floor) separately. Make separate measurements for sections tiled with accent pieces, different colors of tiles, feature strips, and decorative tiles.

For countertops, measure the linear feet of surfaces that will need trim tiles. Count the number of inside and outside corner pieces needed to complete a wall design. If you've design a tiled baseboard to finish your floor design, be sure to include the number of linear feet needed of those tiles.

The amount of each setting material needed also depends on the square footage of the installation. Amounts can be determined by using information found on most product labels.

To be on the safe side, plan to purchase about 10 percent more of all materials—tiles and setting materials—than you actually require to allow for breakage, mistakes, and future needs.

Making the Purchase

Take your square-foot measurements, a design concept, the plan view drawing, and budget guidelines with you when you go shopping for materials. Plan to spend quite a bit of time at the tile showroom or store—you have many decisions to make.

If possible, plan to choose tile on one trip but wait to make your final purchases until you've had some time to think about it. Tile lasts a long time, and a ceramic installation is a major home improvement; you may regret making a purchase on impulse. Some tile outlets may have to order the tile you want, so be sure to allow time for this in your plans, as well.

Most tile installations require the purchase of more than one carton of tiles. Be sure to verify that the tiles in every box are exactly the same color; production runs can vary greatly. If you are installing dimensioned stone, you'll want to check the background colors and the colors of the veins. The same rule applies if you are using colored grout. Buy colored grouts from the same production run and check that the color is the same in every package.

When considering size, be aware that no standard sizing exists within the tile industry. Some tile dimensions are given in centimeters and some in inches. Tile manufacturers are not always exact in their measurements. In addition, some specified tile sizes include the width of the grout

joint, although this is not always clearly stated. Be sure to actually measure a sample tile before estimating your tile needs.

Some decisions must be budgetary ones. Tile prices vary from $1 to $2,000 per square foot, although most tiles sold commercially for residential use are priced between $5 and $10 per square foot. Better-quality clays, longer firing times, and higher firing temperatures make better-quality tiles at a higher price. As this price variation implies, there is a broad spectrum of tile quality. The categories of tiles listed in this chapter indicate quality to some degree. Other quality tests you should make yourself; to do this you'll need a few tiles.

Checking Quality

Once you are fairly certain about which tiles you want, borrow or purchase some samples, including trim tiles if they are to be used, and bring them home. These samples will aid in visualizing how many tiles of each type will be needed to complete the installation. They'll act as a true indicator of color and size in your location and under home lighting, which can be quite different from showroom lights. They will also give you a chance to test the tile's durability under realistic conditions.

Try a scratch test on the sample tiles. If the installation will be a countertop, set a couple of tiles on a table and scrape a pot across them. Is the glaze scratched? Pour some juice on the tiles. Does the liquid soak in immediately? If the tile will be used on a floor, set a few tiles on the floor and run a dress shoe across them. Does the sole leave a mark on the tile? Is the mark difficult to clean off? Then dampen the tile and pull a shoe across it. Does the shoe slip to such an extent that the floor might be dangerous when wet? Does the moisture soak in? These simple tests are important factors in determining the right tile to buy and may make the difference between an installation you are happy with and one that is a problem.

Have Fun

Take your time at the tile store. Experiment with colors, styles, and sizes you didn't plan on using. Keep an open mind to suggestions in product catalogs and showroom displays.

If the tile you like is not correct for use where you intend to install it, the store personnel or the manufacturers' literature should be able to recommend a similar tile that is of the quality you need.

Getting Help

Salespeople in stores that specialize in selling tile are generally well informed about the products they sell.

Tile can also be purchased from architects and designers. These professionals can analyze your needs and help you choose the right tile for your project. They may design the installation, or work with you to achieve a particular look. Tile designers and architects usually work in the same manner as other interior design specialists: You purchase the tile from them at their cost plus a mark-up and/or a design fee.

Basic tile installation is not difficult, but some projects—swimming pools, for example—are best left to professionals. If your tile installation is difficult, or if for one reason or another you choose not to install the tile yourself, hire a licensed tile contractor to do the work. A tile contractor can also advise you on any structural problems and on the need for any

substructure work that must be done prior to tile installation.

The best way to locate a tile contractor is to ask satisfied customers for recommendations. You might ask at your local tile showrooms for recommendations, as well. Before any work begins, be sure to obtain a written estimate including the price for materials (if the contractor will be purchasing them) and the labor costs. If you have definite design ideas, be sure to let the contractor know—before and during installation—so that you end up with the tile job that you wanted and that you paid for.

Ceramic tile is an extremely practical material to use around a stove or fireplace. It is also an ideal material for producing interesting effects. If you don't trust your own sense of design, many tile manufacturers produce panels prearranged in variegated colors.

CERAMIC TILE QUALITY

This section provides information on how tile is manufactured and gives standards by which quality can be judged. This information is presented so that you can determine whether a particular tile is suitable for your installation.

Tile Manufacturing

Ceramic tile has been manufactured for more than six thousand years. Originally, pure clay was dredged from stream- and riverbeds, cleaned of rocks and debris, formed into shape, and left in the sun to dry until hard. These tiles were then used as flooring and as the linings for ovens.

Somewhere along the line, someone realized that the tiles in the ovens were sturdier and more impervious to water than those merely dried in the sun. This discovery led early tile makers to begin baking tiles in their bread ovens; later they began building special ovens called kilns specifically for firing, or baking, tiles.

Another leap in tile history came about when tile makers began to run out of clay and started mixing pottery and old tiles in with the clay to extend the supply. Because pure clay was difficult to obtain, the practice of mixing in various elements caught on quickly and continues today. Besides stretching the clay supply, the additives allowed for varying the tile color.

Today some tile is still made of pure clay, but it is very expensive. Most ceramic tiles are made from a combination of refined clay and ground shale or gypsum, plus talc, vermiculite, and sand; the latter elements control shrinkage. The combination of all these elements and water forms a mixture called a bisque.

The bisque is formed into a tile by one of several different methods, all of which have the same goals: To cast the tile shape and to remove the water from the bisque prior to firing.

Most commercial tile manufacturers use a method known as extrusion. In this method, green (unfired) bisque is squeezed through a press into a die in the shape of a tile.

Smaller manufacturers often use the ramming method to form tiles—pushing the green bisque into a die and stamping it down. Another method of tile formation is to roll the bisque flat and cut the tiles with a form much like a cookie cutter.

Modern craftspeople use a method not unlike that of their ancient predecessors, which is to form the tiles by hand using a wood or metal frame.

Whatever the method of tile formation, the bisque must lose its plasticity before being fired in a kiln. All ceramic tile, whether glazed or unglazed, is fired; some varieties just once, some many times. The purity of the clay, the number of firings, and the temperature of the kiln determine the price of the tile. Because of the cost of energy, tiles that are fired longer and at higher temperatures are more expensive.

Kiln temperatures vary from about 900° to 2,500° F. Lower firing temperatures produce more porous tile and soft glazes; higher temperatures produce dense, non-porous tile and hard glazes.

Kiln time varies from several hours to several days. The less time spent in the kiln, the more porous the tile.

Glazes

The transparent or colored coating on the top side of ceramic tile is called a glaze. Glazes are made up of lead silicates and pigment and are brushed or sprayed onto the surface of the bisque and fired. Glaze can be applied to green bisque and fired with the bisque or applied to fired bisque and fired again.

Unglazed tiles derive their color from the clay. Glazes add color and protect the surface of the tile. Additives are sometimes mixed with glazes to produce textured tiles.

Sawdust is one popular additive; in the kiln the sawdust burns, leaving the tile surface slightly roughened and therefore more slip resistant. Silicon carbide sprinkled on top of the glaze also roughens the surface. Some manufacturers add bits of carbide and stone chips to the glaze to achieve interesting effects.

The hardness of the glaze depends on the temperature of the kiln and the length of time the tile is in the kiln. It is important to know the quality of the glaze when purchasing tiles. Soft glazes, for example, are inappropriate for floors and countertop installations, where everyday use would chip the glaze. These same tiles are perfectly adequate for wall installations, however, where they are less likely to get knocked or bear weight.

Water Absorption

Clay is a moisture-absorbing substance. Glazes repel moisture from the top surface of ceramic tiles, but do not protect the edges and back. Proper tile installation protects substrate from water damage.

Water absorption can lead to cracks in the tile, bacterial growth within the installation, and, eventually, damage to the adhesive and the substrate under the tile.

Tile Quality Standards

The American National Standards Institute (ANSI) measures the water-absorption rates of finished tiles and divides them into four categories. These categories are used as standards for determining the quality of a ceramic tile and whether it is appropriate for a specific installation. Whether the tile is glazed or unglazed has no effect on the measured water-absorption rate.

It is important to understand this rating system so that you use the right type of tile in the right location. For example, porous tile is perfectly suitable for use in dry interior locations such as hallways, where the use of costlier less-porous tile is not necessary. However, exterior installations in cold climates require nonporous tiles. A guide to the types of tile recommended for various locations appears on pages 26 and 27.

There is no difference in the procedures used when working with tiles in different categories; all are laid out in the same manner and cut and installed using the same tools, materials, and techniques. The minor differences between them are listed below.

Nonvitreous Tiles

These very porous tiles absorb more than 7 percent of their weight in water. They are fired at a low temperature for only a short time—usually about 2,100° F for 18 hours or so. Nonvitreous tiles are not a good choice for wet areas (around sinks or as shower or tub surrounds) or for exterior installations in cold areas. They are not freeze-thaw stable, which means they will absorb moisture and crack when the moisture freezes and expands. Nonvitreous

tiles are generally the least expensive tiles available.

Install nonvitreous tile using standard thinsetting techniques and organic mastic or any thinset adhesive. If you mix the adhesive yourself, make it slightly more liquid than you would normally to make up for the water absorbency of the tile. Be sure to completely moisten the unglazed areas of the tiles prior to grouting to prevent them from absorbing the liquid in the grout and causing it to cure too quickly.

If you have no choice and must install nonvitreous tile in a wet area, use proper waterproofing techniques and a latex additive in both the thinset adhesive and the grout.

Semi-vitreous Tile

Fired at the same temperature but for a longer time than nonvitreous tiles, semi-vitreous tiles absorb between 3 and 7 percent of their weight in water. If properly installed, semi-vitreous tiles can be used in any interior location—even wet areas—but should not be used in exterior locations in cold climates since they are not freeze-thaw stable.

Install semi-vitreous tiles with organic mastic or any thinset adhesive using standard thinsetting techniques. As with nonvitreous tiles, be sure to completely moisten the unglazed areas prior to grouting.

Vitreous Tile

The best all-around tiles for residential use, vitreous tiles are very dense, having been fired at 2,200° F for 24 hours or more. Vitreous tiles absorb only between 0.5 and 3 percent of their weight in water. Use vitreous tiles anywhere, in both interior and exterior locations and in wet or dry installations. Vitreous tiles are strong and can withstand heavy loads without breaking, making them ideal for use on floors and hearths.

Install vitreous tiles with organic mastic or any thinset adhesive in dry areas and with any thinset adhesive in wet installations. Because of the

low absorption rate, you only need to sponge the unglazed areas of tiles before grouting.

Impervious Tile

Fired at 2,500° F for anywhere from 25 to 60 hours, impervious tiles are nearly waterproof. They absorb less than 0.5 percent of their weight in water. These tiles are top-of-the-line products that are rarely used in residential installations but are often found in hospitals, labs, and commercial applications where cleanliness is important. Unlike other grades of ceramic tile, impervious tiles can be sterilized.

Impervious tiles are installed in the same manner as other tiles. Use any organic mastic or thinset adhesive for installations that will not be exposed to water and any thinset adhesive in wet installations. Because of their low absorption rate, there is no need to wet these tiles prior to grouting.

Testing Vitreosity

It is important to know the water-absorption rate of any tile prior to installation. Not all manufacturers list this information on product labels, and if you find loose tiles (perhaps left in your garage by a friendly previous owner) you won't know what type they are. The characteristics of various types of glazed and unglazed tiles can sometimes provide a clue as to the quality of a tile.

The best way to determine the water-absorption rate of a tile is to test it yourself. To do this, turn the tile over, pour a little water on it, and wait a couple of minutes. If the water sits on the tile back, the tile is vitreous; if it soaks in a little, it is semi-vitreous; if it soaks in as if the tile were a sponge, it is nonvitreous.

A Shopping Guide

This chart should serve as a handy guide when shopping for suitable tile and setting materials. The guide lists only ceramic tile products. Dimensioned stone is usually categorized as semi-vitreous or vitreous floor tile and can be installed anywhere these types of tiles would be suitable.

The adhesive and grout categories are very broad. Before purchasing a product, be sure to read manufacturer's directions for exact recommendations.

Location	Tile Type	Adhesive	Grout	Comments
Entrance hall	Unglazed or glazed, textured semi-vitreous or vitreous floor tile	Epoxy thinset over wood backing; any thinset over other backings	Portland cement or sand-portland cement grout	Consider slip resistance of tile. Check use of latex thinset adhesive over plywood backing.
Stair tread	Unglazed or glazed, textured semi-vitreous or vitreous floor tile	Epoxy thinset over wood backing; any thinset over other backings	Portland cement or sand-portland cement grout	Set tread tiles after riser tiles.
Stair riser	Any tile; should be thin enough to adhere well to a vertical surface	Organic mastic; any thinset adhesive	Portland cement or sand-portland cement grout	Individual tiles do not need to be grouted.
Kitchen floor	Glazed semi-vitreous or vitreous floor tile	Epoxy thinset over wood backing or existing resilient flooring. Any thinset adhesive over other backings	Portland cement or sand-portland cement grout	Unglazed tiles and light-colored stone tiles are not stain resistant; use caution in heavily used kitchens.
Countertop with sink	Glazed semi-vitreous or vitreous tile	Epoxy thinset over wood backing; latex or acrylic thinset adhesive over other backings	Grouts with latex or acrylic additives	Sealers should not be used on tiles in food-preparation areas.
Countertop without sink	Unglazed or glazed, non-vitreous, semi-vitreous, or vitreous tiles	Organic mastic; any thinset adhesive	Portland cement grout	Consider use when choosing an unglazed countertop tile.
Backsplash	Any tile; should be thin enough to adhere well to a vertical surface	Any thinset adhesive	Grouts with latex or acrylic additives	Use glazed tile on backsplashes behind sinks.
Bathroom floor	Glazed semi-vitreous or vitreous floor tile. Textured tiles recommended	Epoxy thinset over wood backing or existing resilient flooring; any thinset adhesive over other backings	Grouts with latex or acrylic additives	Consider slip resistance when wet.
Tub surround	Any glazed tile suitable for vertical installation	Latex and acrylic thinset adhesives	Grouts with latex or acrylic additives	Consider slip resistance when wet.
Shower wall	Glazed semi-vitreous or vitreous tile; unglazed mosaic	Latex and acrylic thinset adhesives; epoxy thinsets	Grouts with latex or acrylic additives	Check water-resistance of marble tiles before installing them in wet areas.
Shower floor	Glazed and textured vitreous tile; unglazed mosaic	Latex and acrylic thinset adhesives; epoxy thinsets	Grouts with latex or acrylic additives	Slip resistance and water-resistance are prime concerns. Be sure substrate meets local building codes.

Location	Tile Type	Adhesive	Grout	Comments
Interior walls	Any tile; should be thin enough to adhere well to a vertical surface	Organic mastic; epoxy thinset over wood backings; any thinset adhesive over other backings	Portland cement or sand-portland cement grout	Do not use organic mastics in wet areas.
Fireplace surround	Any tile; should be thin enough to adhere well to a vertical surface	Water-mixed thinset adhesives	Portland cement or sand-portland cement grout	Check local codes governing firewalls near fireplaces and wood stoves.
Hearth	Any floor tile; avoid tiles with soft—easily scratched—glazes	Epoxy thinset over wood backings; water-mixed thinset over other backings	Portland cement or sand-portland cement grout	Check local codes governing materials used near open fireplaces.
Family room floor	Glazed or unglazed, semi-vitreous or vitreous floor tile	Epoxy thinset over wood backings or existing resilient flooring; water-mixed thinset over other backings	Portland cement or sand-portland cement grout	Consider the stain-resisting benefits of glazed tile if food and beverages will be served in the room.
Window/door surround	Any tile; look for specialty pieces made for windowsills	Organic mastic; any thinset adhesive	Portland cement or sand-portland cement grout	Do not use organic mastics for exterior installations.
Garden path (temperate)	Any unglazed tile	Water-mixed, latex, or acrylic thinset adhesives	Sand-portland cement grout	Check for slip resistance.
Garden path (freeze-thaw)	Unglazed vitreous tile	Latex or acrylic thinset adhesives	Sand-portland cement grout	Slope ground so that melting snow drains away.
Patio (temperate)	Any unglazed tile	Water-mixed, latex, or acrylic thinset adhesives	Sand-portland cement grout	Check for slip resistance.
Patio (freeze-thaw)	Unglazed vitreous tile	Latex or acrylic thinset adhesives	Sand-portland cement grout	Slope ground so that melting snow drains away.
Fountain	Glazed semi-vitreous or vitreous tiles	Epoxy thinset	Dry-set grout	Install a drain so that fountain can be cleaned.
Pool surround	Glazed and textured vitreous tile	Epoxy thinset	Dry-set grout	Pool tiles should be installed by a licensed professional.
Exterior walls	Glazed or unglazed, semi-vitreous or vitreous tiles	Water-mixed thinset adhesives	Portland cement or sand-portland cement grout	Make sure that wall is smooth and properly prepared.
Signage	Any tile; should be thin enough to adhere well to a vertical surface	Organic mastic; any thinset adhesive	Any grout	Consider attaching tiles to a plywood backing, which is then attached to the wall.

CERAMIC VARIETIES

The most noticeable feature of any ceramic tile is its finish: The color or colors, the shape, and the glaze—if it is glazed. Although color, shape, and glaze are important design considerations, the choice of tile should depend more on the suitability of a specific type of tile for a particular location.

In this section, you will find descriptions of a variety of ceramic tile and stone products.

The ANSI tile standards discussed previously are the determining factors. When you enter a tile store, however, you won't see tiles displayed according to their vitreosity. What you will see are hundreds of varieties of glazed and unglazed ceramics.

Glazed Tiles

Glazed tiles are those with a top coat, usually colored, that is sprayed onto the bisque and fired. Glazed finishes are either high-gloss, semi-matte, matte, or textured. The quality, or hardness, of the glaze is determined by the length of time in the kiln and the temperature of the firing. Some glazes are fired more than once. Multiple colors in a glaze are applied separately but fired at the same time. The number of firings and the temperature of the kiln are reflected in the price of the tile.

Glazed tiles are classified as either wall, floor, or countertop tiles and are sold loose or mounted on sheets as panels and mosaics.

Tile Backs

While you're admiring the tops of the tiles, you must also investigate their backs. Tile backs vary greatly, and they indicate several important facts about how and where the tile was made and where it can be used.

Some tile backs are ridged. These ridges indicate that the tile was probably made using an extrusion method. The ridges expand the surface area of the tile back, which will allow it to hold more adhesive and will make for a better-quality bond. Ridge-backed tiles are usually vitreous or impervious and are especially well suited for use on floors and heavily used countertops.

Other tile backs are covered with buttons or dots. Button-backed tiles were probably pressed and then stacked in the kiln for firing. Most button-backed tiles are nonvitreous or semi-vitreous. When installed, they do not adhere as well to the substrate as do ridged or flat-backed tiles. Because air can remain in the spaces between the buttons and cause the tiles to shift when stepped on, button-backed tiles are best used on vertical surfaces or on lightly used countertops.

Most tiles sold today for residential use are flat backed. These tiles are also made by the pressing method but are fired at a higher temperature than button-backed tiles and so are harder, usually semi-vitreous or vitreous. Use flat-backed tiles for any ceramic installation.

Tile backs often supply other important information. Many manufacturers stamp their name, the production number, the name of the color, and the country of origin right on the back of the tile. This information is valuable when purchasing more than one box of tiles and helpful if you need to replace any tiles during rejuvenation projects.

Another difference you may notice between tiles is that some have small protrusions on the sides. These lugs control spacing when tiles are set.

Wall Tiles

Glazed wall tiles are usually nonvitreous tiles made from a gypsum mixture coated with a soft glaze. These tiles are most often produced by the pressing method and have flat or button backs. Wall tiles are commonly ¼ inch thick and anywhere from 4 to 12 inches square. Standard wall tiles are intended for interior use only as they are not freeze-thaw stable. All styles of glazes can be found on wall tiles, from high-gloss to textured.

Floor Tiles

Glazed floor tiles come in nonvitreous, semi-vitreous, vitreous, and impervious grades and are made from a clay-mixture bisque and coated with a hard glaze. Floor tiles should be at least ½ inch thick; their sizes vary up to about 12 inches square. The grade of tile used depends on the location of the installation. The glazes found on floor tiles vary from semi-matte to matte; most floor tiles are textured for slip resistance.

Countertop Tiles

Tiles approved for use on kitchen countertops and bathroom vanities can also be used on shelves, windowsills, tabletops, and as decorative inserts. Glazed tiles for countertops should be semi-vitreous or vitreous and at least ½ inch thick. A wide range of countertop trim tiles are available to match or contrast with countertop-tile colors and patterns.

Mounted Tiles

Ceramic tiles that are mounted, evenly spaced, on a backing sheet are called mounted tiles or tile panels. Various kinds of tiles are sold in this manner, both full-sized tiles and tile mosaics. Most mounted tiles are vitreous. Depending on the glaze, mounted tiles are appropriate for use on walls, floors, and countertops. The backing material can be paper, plastic mesh, or a grid of rubber buttons.

Face-mounted tiles, as the name implies, are held together with a paper mounting sheet that is affixed to the face of the tiles. The paper is left in place during setting and is dampened and removed after the adhesive has dried. Back-mounted tiles are held together by plastic mesh applied to the tile backs. The mesh is left in place when the tile is set. Dot-mounted tiles are connected by rubber or plastic buttons; these are also left in place when tile is set. The advantage of back- and dot-mounted tiles over face-mounted tiles is that you can see where you are setting the tiles during installation.

Mounted-tile sheets are usually purchased in 1- to 3-foot squares; the tiles themselves are commonly 4 to 6 inches square. They may all be the same color, but often these tiles are already set into patterns that you can then repeat over the run of your installation. Others have interesting shapes or combinations of shapes that fit together perfectly. Many manufacturers offer individual tiles to match their mounted tiles, which you can use to complete your installation.

Install mounted tiles in the same manner as loose tiles. Use thinset adhesive (avoid organic mastic because the mastic doesn't adhere very well to the backing) and standard thinsetting techniques.

Mounted tiles provide several advantages over loose tiles with regard to setting. Foremost is that the grout joints are already established. Because of that and because of the large format of a sheet, the tile is faster to install. However, you must take care to match the spacing between sheets to the grout joints between tiles.

A disadvantage of mounted tiles is that the backing materials may impair the quality of the bond between the tile and the adhesive. Mounted tiles are also more expensive than their loose-tile equivalents.

Mosaics

By definition mosaics are tiles that are 2 inches or smaller across. Mosaics are usually made of high-quality clay that is fired for a long time at a high temperature. They are vitreous, quite dense, and freeze-thaw stable. Mosaics are good for use on walls, floors, countertops, and other tile projects in both wet and dry locations, indoors and outdoors.

Mosaic tiles are almost always sold back-mounted on mesh sheets, although you can usually purchase loose mosaic tiles by special order. Install mosaics using thinset adhesive and standard thinsetting techniques. Because of the numerous joints, you'll need more grout to cover a mosaic-tile installation than you would for an equal-sized installation of larger tiles.

Decorated Tiles

Tiles can be decorated in addition to being glazed. Some decorated tiles are hand-painted; others have decals attached. Hand-painted tiles are created by craftspeople who paint on the surface of a tile and then fire it. Painted tiles are generally too fragile for use on heavily used floors and countertops, but can be used architecturally or as accents to walls, backsplashes, fireplace surrounds, and the like. They can be used individually or in groups that form a pattern. Decorated tiles are often used in signs.

Hand-painted tiles are sold in tile stores, at artists' studios, and often at crafts fairs and art shows. Common themes are animals and plants, and often several tiles can be arranged to show a scenario such as a basket of flowers or a country scene. Many tile artists have samples that you can choose from, and will also customize tiles for your installation.

Consider having an artist create accent tiles especially for you. These might depict anything from a family coat of arms to a company logo. Artists can also paint tiles to match wallpaper, fabric, or a china pattern. The use of hand-painted tiles as accents or in a pattern adds a wonderful variety to decorating with ceramic tiles.

If you purchase hand-painted tiles to put into a run of commercially produced tiles, make sure that the thickness of all tiles is the same. If you are having custom work done, take a sample of your tile to the artist and discuss the use of a painted tile in conjunction with commercial tiles.

Decal tiles are less expensive than hand-painted tiles, and are also quite attractive. Also, you can attach them to the tiles you are using. For painted tiles, you must find blanks that match those selected for the main installation. Sample decals are usually available at tile stores; common themes are flowers, animals, vegetables, and graphic symbols and motifs. Often you can put together a group of decals to make a pattern, such as a vine with flowers. This can be used as a stripe across a backsplash or as a trim around a countertop. Once you choose the decal, it is applied to a glazed tile and fired.

Decals are fragile and should be confined to tiles that will be installed on walls and lightly used areas of countertops.

Trim Tiles

Trim pieces and accessory tiles, such as cove and bullnose tiles, are used to turn corners, edge countertops, fit around fixtures, and act as finishing pieces. These and other specialty ceramics are manufactured in the same manner as other glazed tiles.

A wide variety of trim tiles is available to match various tile colors and patterns. If no trim tiles are available to match the tile you have chosen, consider using trim pieces that contrast with your tile to make a pattern. The many types of trim tiles and the places in which to use them are illustrated on page 37.

Unglazed Tiles

Unglazed tiles have no baked-on coating. The color of the tile is the same throughout the entire tile body and is determined by the natural clay, shale, or combination of elements that make up the bisque. In some cases pigments are added to the bisque prior to firing. This extends the number of colors available. The most common types of unglazed tiles are pavers, brick veneers, and quarry tiles. All are sold as loose tiles.

Pavers

Pavers are unglazed tiles made of clay, shale, or porcelain, by hand or by machine. They are at least ½ inch thick and are suitable for use on floors and walls. Colors range from terra-cotta to yellow to brown. Pavers are available in squares, rectangles, hexagons, octagons, and a variety of other shapes. They are often paired with smaller tiles, one or two inches square, called spots. These accent spots may be glazed or colored with pigment, and extend the design possibilities of pavers considerably.

No need to balance the vacuum on these stairs. They can be easily maintained by just dusting or sweeping.

Machine-made pavers. Pavers made by machine using the extrusion method are vitreous and are generally ⅝ inch thick. Use these tiles in interior and exterior locations and in both wet and dry installations.

Pavers should be sealed to protect the tile and retard wear. Many pavers are already sealed, but if the ones you purchase are not, coat them with a penetrating sealer before and after grouting.

Machine-made pavers are dense enough for use on countertops, but should not be used on countertops in food-preparation areas. The sealer necessary to protect them is not recommended for use near food.

Handmade pavers. Often called Mexican tiles, handmade pavers may be the closest tiles found today to those made centuries ago. They are nonvitreous and come in a wide range of dimensions. Thicknesses run from ½ to 2 inches, often within the same box of tiles. Handmade tiles are very distinctive: You'll often find fingerprints, stones, straw, and other debris cast into the paver.

Handmade pavers can be used on interior floors in dry locations and on exterior floors in warm climates. They are too porous for wet locations and are not freeze-thaw stable. Most handmade pavers are too thick to use on walls; the adhesive just won't hold them vertically. Handmade pavers are not flat and are too unstable and too porous for use on countertops.

Due to the difficulties involved in working with handmade pavers, consider using machine-made pavers (which actually look very much like their traditional counterparts) instead. Or hire a licensed contractor experienced in handmade paver installation to do the job for you.

Brick Veneers

Several different products are sold as brick veneers. Some are actually just thin bricks. Others are made from tile bisque ingredients and fired at a low temperature. Still others are formed bisque that is dried but not fired.

Brick veneers simulate real brick. They are usually about ½ inch thick and as wide and long as regular bricks. All are extremely porous.

Brick veneer can be installed either inside or outside. Check the manufacturer's specifications for use of bisque-style brick veneers; they are often too soft for use anywhere but on walls.

Installing brick veneer is a clever way to cover a concrete-slab patio or path or to face a cement-block retaining wall. Outside, use standard thinsetting techniques and install using any thinset adhesive. Inside, use either a thinset adhesive or an organic mastic.

Quarry Tiles

Originally, tiles made from quarried stone, which was cut, ground, and polished, were called quarry tiles. These tiles were extremely expensive, so a method was developed of making a semi-vitreous or vitreous clay tile by extrusion that would mimic the hard quality of stone. These tiles came to be called quarry tiles. Tiles that are made out of true quarried stone are categorized as dimensioned stone (see page 32).

The products called quarry tiles are very hard, unglazed tiles that range in color from tan to deep red to black. They are usually square, rectangular, or hexagonal, from 4 to 12 inches in diameter, and ½ to ¾ inch thick. Install quarry tiles using standard thinsetting techniques and any thinset adhesive.

Use quarry tiles indoors in dry locations. If properly sealed, they can also be used outdoors and in wet locations. Quarry tiles can be installed on walls, floors, and countertops, except countertops in food-preparation areas. (The sealers required to protect the tiles should not be used in areas where food will be prepared.) Seal with a coating sealer and allow to dry prior to grouting.

DIMENSIONED STONE

Dimensioned-stone tiles are made from marble, slate, granite, and other natural materials. Quarried in all parts of the world, dimensioned stone has many architectural uses.

Traditionally, architects and designers have considered natural stone to be massive, expensive, and difficult to install. Stone is often seen in large-scale commercial and government projects and in expensive residences.

In the 1970s, however, major breakthroughs changed the processing of stone. The result is a uniform, lightweight, and economical veneer product that can be used in homes of every size and style. These dimensioned-stone tiles are most often finished into pieces that are 12 inches square and ⅜ inch thick.

Types of Stone

The many types of dimensioned stone vary in look and price, but installation and care guidelines for all of them are similar. These guidelines are not very different from those for ceramic tiles.

Dimensioned stone is available in three different finishes: polished, honed, and flamed. Polished stone, most often used on walls and interior floors, has a rich, shiny finish that looks something like a glaze.

Honed stone has a smooth finish; it looks like what you might imagine the natural rock looks like when it comes out of the ground. Honed tiles are a practical choice for floors because

they do not show the wear of foot traffic. If properly sealed, honed tiles can be used in wet areas where polished tiles would be dangerously slick.

Flamed stone (also called torched by some manufacturers) has a rough finish that is particularly valuable in high-traffic areas, both interior and exterior, where a slip-resistant surface is desired. The finish is achieved by sand-blasting.

Marble

For more than two thousand years, marble has been the material of choice for many of the world's greatest buildings. The Taj Mahal, the Parthenon, and the United States Capitol, as well as many fine commercial buildings and residences have elegant marble interiors and exteriors.

Marble is limestone that has been changed through the actions of heat, pressure, and time deep beneath the earth's surface. The result is a hard composition of crystals that develop a characteristic veining. Colors range from almost pure white to nearly black. Colored marble occurs due to the presence of minerals and other matter within the rock.

Marble is hard and durable, and should be considered for use in the same areas as semi-vitreous ceramic tile. There are some problems inherent in the natural product, however. Generally, the more heavily veined the marble, the weaker it will be.

Wear will be most noticeable in darker colors such as black. Highly colored marble—green, brown, and black—may fade in sunlight. The darker the marble, the more noticeable this fading will be. To get an idea of what the tile will look like after fading, examine the back side. Constant traffic will eventually wear away the finish of polished marble; severity of wear depends on the amount of traffic and the hardness of the marble. The shine can be restored by repolishing—a job that should be done by professionals.

Granite

Harder even than marble, granite is incredibly durable, can be used in interior and exterior installations, and is easy to maintain—even with heavy use. Granite has the density and freeze-thaw stability of vitreous ceramic tile. It is part of the earth's crust—igneous rock composed of crystals of feldspar, quartz, and other minerals such as mica and augite. Granite is present all over the world; each deposit has its own distinctive characteristics and color.

Although polished granite is very durable, some of the softer granites will eventually show wear after constant use. Repolishing granite requires professional equipment.

Slate

Slate is a handsome but brittle material with an easily identifiable veining. It is usually found in various shades of gray, with tints ranging from blue to dark purple to black. It can be used in both interior and exterior installations, although dark-colored slate will fade when constantly exposed to sunlight. Slate is available in uniformly shaped tiles and in irregular pieces, which are often used in patios. Slate installed in wet and exterior locations should be sealed.

Travertine

Quarried originally in France, travertine is a mineral consisting of layers of calcium carbonate formed by underground deposits near spring waters and hot springs. Travertine is rarer than some of the other dimensioned stone, and often more expensive.

The master bathroom is usually small enough and private enough to indulge in a little fantasy. Here, a "skyline" of slate towers is outlined against a cloudy, pink "sky."

Above: *Tile can be highlighted by contrasting it with other materials. Here, the color and texture of slate-tiled risers are set off against smooth, polished wood treads.*
Opposite: *Cast stone is an interesting new product that is not widely available. However, the idea of quoining a room can be imitated in other materials.*

Terrazzo

Not technically a dimensioned stone, terrazzo consists of small pieces of marble or granite set in mortar and highly polished. Traditionally, terrazzo was used in large applications and was installed by professionals. More recently it has become available in precast tiles, which are usually available where dimensioned stone is sold. Terrazzo tiles can be used on floors and walls.

Uses for Dimensioned Stone

Most types of dimensioned stone can be used on floors and walls in both interior and exterior locations. Common uses include entryway floors, bath and shower surrounds, hearths, fireplace surrounds, kitchen and bathroom floors, paths, and patios. Dimensioned stone should not be used overhead as it is too heavy for a guaranteed bond. Stone slabs, which are often available to match dimensioned-stone tiles, can be used for countertops.

When designing patterns of dimensioned-stone tiles that include more than one type, finish, or color, make sure that the various products are compatible in terms of wear, care, and slip resistance.

Buying Dimensioned Stone

Since dimensioned stone is a natural product, the quality can't be ensured by standards like those applied to manufactured ceramic tiles. When shopping, be aware of the inconsistencies that naturally occur.

Tiles are usually sorted by background color but veins and markings vary greatly from tile to tile. In fact, although many are similar, no two are exactly alike.

When buying these tiles, look first at the background color. Next, check the veining and marking. Check every box of tile you buy to make sure that tiles are not wildly different.

Before purchasing tiles, check them for density, strength, and—if they will be used near a fireplace or wood-burning stove—for heat-transfer capacity. Avoid tiles with a very rough surface as they will be difficult to keep clean. However, if they will be used on the floor, make sure the surface of the tiles is rough enough to prevent slipping.

TRIM TILE

Whereas tiles for the main installation are flat and glazed on one side only, trim tiles are glazed on one or more sides and are shaped to overhang edges and wrap around corners.

Trim tiles come in a variety of shapes, sizes, colors, and patterns often matching field tiles. If the manufacturer of your chosen tile does not offer matching trim tiles, check out other lines. As long as field and trim tiles match in dimension, you can mix an installation. Depending on your design, you may want to purchase trim tiles that contrast the field tiles.

If you can't find anything suitable, there are alternatives to ceramic trim tiles. Wood trims, plastic edging strips, and metal edges are available to complete tile installations.

There are no trim tiles to match unglazed tile or dimensioned-stone tile but if tiles are fairly soft—pavers for example—you can round out edges by rubbing with a masonry stone or small hand grinder. Be sure to seal the newly formed edge.

A counter should be finished with trim tiles to hide the edge of the installation and the substrate beneath. Note how the high contrast between grout and tile necessitates a well-executed installation. Dark grout paired with light-colored tiles accentuates the grid, making every joint visible and any crooked line more noticeable.

Where to Use Trim Tile

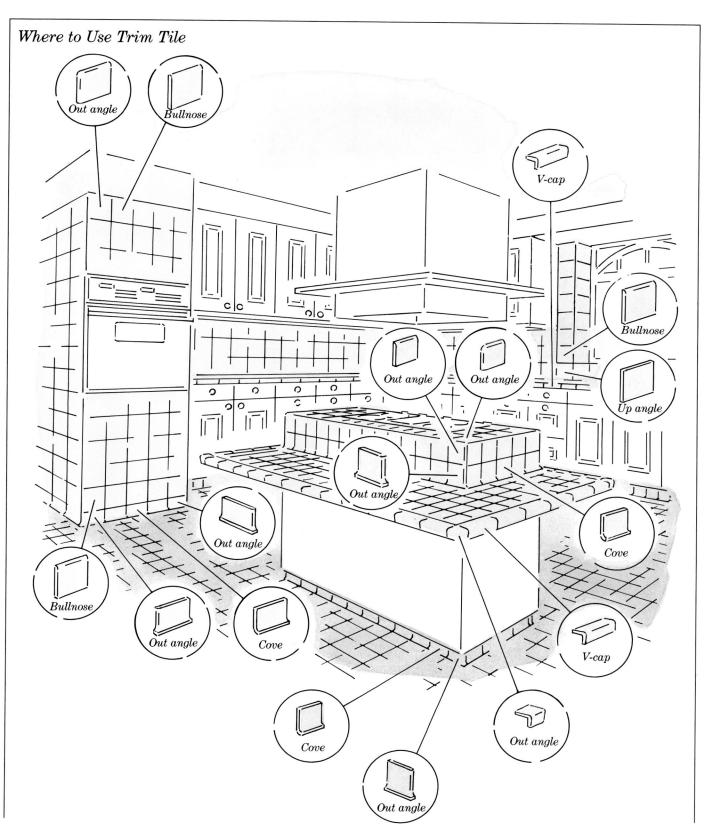

Out angle

Bullnose

V-cap

Bullnose

Out angle

Out angle

Up angle

Out angle

Cove

Out angle

Bullnose

Out angle

Cove

V-cap

Cove

Out angle

Out angle

SURFACE PREPARATION

Behind every good tile installation there is a good surface. A beautiful design, lovely tile, and a careful setting job will all be for naught if the base is unsound or badly prepared.

Tile should be installed over a firm surface, or substrate. If the substrate flexes when only slight pressure is applied, replace and strengthen it before installing tile. Any movement in the floor after the tile is set in place may cause tile to crack. All surfaces should be sound, clean, and dry before tile is installed.

In addition to being structurally sound, surfaces to be tiled must also be flat and level. An uneven substrate will result in a tile installation with an uneven surface. Use a spirit level to check whether floors and countertops are level. Check in several locations. A difference of 1/8 inch over a span of 10 feet is acceptable.

If the tile installation is part of a new construction project, make sure the carpenters know which areas will be tiled. Check at the framing stage to make sure walls are plumb and square and joists are installed in such a way that there will not be problems in areas where a tiled floor meets another finish flooring material.

Suitable Substrates

Ceramic tile can be installed over a wide range of newly installed or existing surfaces.

Ceramic Tile

Existing tile can serve as a substrate on which to set new tile. Check that the existing installation is in good condition and that there are no cracks. Use a masonry rubbing stone to roughen the existing tile; this will remove the glaze and provide a good bonding surface. If the level of the grout joints is lower than the surface of the tiles, be sure to fill and level gaps with adhesive.

Several adhesives are suitable for installing tile over tile; check product labels.

Sheet Paneling

This type of paneling (usually covered with a wood-grain veneer) is too thin and too flexible to mount tile on. Remove it and replace with cementitious backer units (CBU, see opposite page), plywood, or wallboard.

Cement Mortar

Also called portland cement or mud, concrete mortar is the traditional substrate for tile installation. "Deck mud"—cement mortar for floors and countertops—varies slightly in composition from "wall mud."

New installations. Cement mortar is suitable for most surfaces and installations when properly prepared. It can be installed over brick, stone, concrete, wood or steel stud framing, foam insulation board, wallboard, rough wood, plywood, or plaster. If waterproofed, cement mortar can be used in areas exposed to moisture.

Cement mortar is long lasting and will withstand considerable weight. Most importantly, it can be shaped to correct a setting surface that is out of plumb, out of level, or badly flawed. It can also be shaped to allow for curved or other specialty designs.

Although a cement-mortar bed makes an excellent substrate for walls, floors, and heavily used countertops, it is tricky to install. Mortar is messy and heavy, and, because it sets fast, must be installed quickly. Modern materials, specifically CBU, have made mortar beds unnecessary for most residential tile installations.

If the surface or design precludes the use of anything but a cement-mortar substrate, consider hiring a professional to lay the bed, and then install the tile yourself.

Concrete Slab

If it is smooth, flat, dry, clean, and free of cracks, a concrete slab makes an excellent base for a tile floor.

New installations. New slabs should be reinforced with wire mesh or reinforcing bar; check local building codes for requirements. Finish with a wood float or brush with a broom so that the surface is rough. Allow new concrete to cure for at least 28 days before setting tile. For wet installations, apply a waterproofing membrane between the concrete and the adhesive.

Existing installations. Check that an existing concrete slab is flat and level. Fill any holes or low spots with concrete or tile-setting adhesive. If the slab has a smooth finish, roughen it with a rubbing stone or electric grinder. Grind off any high spots.

If you will be laying large pavers, small depressions in the surface won't matter. If laying smaller tiles, prepare the surface more carefully.

Be sure to remove all grease, paint, excess concrete, and other foreign materials from existing concrete and vacuum thoroughly before applying adhesive.

If the existing slab is glossy and does not absorb water, it may have been treated with a curing or acceleration compound or a form-releasing agent that will prevent the adhesive from bonding. Sandblasting the slab may help, but the chemicals may still prevent good adhesion. If you encounter this problem, or if the concrete slab is cracked, very uneven, or generally in bad condition, consider pouring a new concrete surface over the existing one.

If there are small cracks in the concrete, consider installing an isolation membrane (see page 41) to prevent future damage to the tile. Large or active cracks are often caused by tree roots or a shifting foundation. Isolate and eliminate the cause before repairing the effects.

Cementitious Backer Units
Developed specifically for tile installation, CBU is a backer board composed of concrete mortar covered on both sides with reinforcing fiberglass mesh. This board is rigid and strong, and provides an excellent surface for tile installation. Some CBU brands are not affected by water and can be used for both dry and wet installations on walls and countertops. Some brands can also be used on floors.

CBU for interior use is manufactured in panels that are either 3 or 4 feet wide, 4 to 8 feet long, and $1/4$, $7/16$, or $1/2$ inch thick. The panels weigh between $2^1/2$ and 4 pounds per square foot. Exterior-grade CBU is 4 feet wide, 8 feet long, and $1/2$ inch thick.

Most types of CBU should be nailed or screwed to an underlay. They should not be attached directly to joists or studs. Always follow the manufacturer's recommendation.

Installing CBU
Cut CBU with a utility knife in the same manner as wallboard: Score sheets on the coated side then snap them. Precut pieces, making necessary cutouts, then nail or screw them in place using $1^1/2$-inch galvanized or rust-resistant nails or $1^1/4$-inch galvanized coarse-thread, sharp-point screws. Drive the fasteners flush with the coated surface but do not countersink them. When attaching CBU over wallboard, be sure to use fasteners long enough to penetrate

through the wallboard and into the studs.

To prevent any moisture seeping through, seal all joints and cutouts by embedding two-inch, glass mesh tape in a latex thinset adhesive. (Use this same adhesive when tiling over CBU.) All edges and corners must be covered with three layers of fiberglass-mesh tape embedded in a thin coat of mortar. Allow adhesive to dry before installing the tile.

Although most CBU's are unaffected by moisture, install a waterproofing membrane over them for wet installations.

Linoleum and Resilient Flooring
Tile can be set over uncushioned linoleum, sheet vinyl, or vinyl tiles with a minimum amount of surface preparation. As long as the existing surface is sound and clean, dry-installation tile work should go smoothly. If tiles have lifted due to moisture or some other problem, remove tiles, eliminate the problem, and repair substrate before proceeding.

Cushioned sheet flooring should be removed because it flexes too much and may cause the tile or grout to crack.

Avoid installing tile over multiple layers of sheet flooring. The weight of the tile may cause the layers to compress, cracking the grout.

Before installing new tile, repair any loose or damaged areas. Scrub the surface with a cleanser strong enough to remove all wax, grease, and dirt. Roughen flooring with abrasive paper and vacuum thoroughly before applying the adhesive.

For dry installations, use an epoxy thinset adhesive or a compatible latex thinset. For wet installations, remove the sheet flooring and install a suitable waterproof underlayment.

Caution. Be extremely careful if you suspect that the flooring is vinyl asbestos. When flooring is removed or sanded, asbestos fibers will be released into the air. If you have this type of floor, either cover it with plywood or hire a licensed asbestos-removal company to remove it.

Lumber
Board lumber and construction lumber are not suitable substrates for tile. Humidity changes cause wood to expand and contract, and the movement may crack tile and grout. Cover a lumber floor with plywood or CBU to ensure a successful tile installation.

Masonry Walls
If prepared correctly, concrete block, brick, and stucco walls make excellent bases for tile installation. If the wall is flat and free of cracks, apply tile with latex thinset. If the wall is dimpled with indentations deeper than $1/4$ inch, first mix some thinset to the consistency of thick paint and apply it to smooth out the area to be tiled.

Potential cracking problems can be prevented by installing an isolation membrane. For wet installations, apply a waterproofing membrane.

Paint
As long as a painted wall is sound and not made of an unsuitable material such as sheet paneling, it can be tiled over.

Before tiling a painted wall, remove all loose paint and roughen the surface with abrasive paper. Clean the wall and wipe away dust with a damp rag. Do not use chemical paint removers because they may have an adverse effect on the adhesive.

Particleboard
Because particleboard tends to expand and contract with changes in humidity, it is not a recommended substrate for tile. Particleboard surfaces should be either removed and replaced with plywood or covered with CBU.

Plaster Walls
Plaster that is hard, flat, and uncracked makes a good setting surface for tile. Treat these walls in the

same manner as masonry walls. If the plaster is soft and crumbles when poked, it is probably made up primarily of lime and should be replaced with wallboard or CBU before tiling.

Plastic Laminate

Existing plastic laminate makes a fine substrate for ceramic tile. It is flat, solid, and waterproof. To prepare the surface for tiling, clean the laminate, remove all grease and dirt, and then roughen the surface with abrasive paper. Be sure any loose laminate is firmly glued down, and fill in any gaps or cracks with epoxy adhesive.

Use epoxy adhesive directly over the laminate as a setting material.

Plywood

Plywood is a sturdy substrate commonly used under tile on floors and countertops. It can be used in new construction or to cover existing surfaces that are not suitable for tiling.

New installations. Purchase plywood that is exterior grade (AXC) or better. Marine grade is superior but can be quite expensive. Interior-grade plywood is not recommended because it is laminated with glues that are not waterproof.

Carefully inspect every sheet before purchase. Discard any boards that are warped or have wood resin on the surface.

When fastening plywood to another material, countersink nail or screw heads. Sand off any wood fibers that protrude above the surface, and vacuum well to remove dust before tiling.

Use an epoxy thinset adhesive with plywood in dry installations. For a wet installation, waterproof the plywood and use an epoxy, latex, or acrylic thinset adhesive.

Existing installations. If you already have a plywood substrate that is in good shape, be sure to sand off waxes, oils, varnish, and paint, and vacuum up the dust prior to applying adhesive.

Sheet Metal

Sheet metal on countertops and pre-fabricated fireboxes can be used as a substrate as long as it does not flex. If the sheet metal has too much flex, clean it and attach CBU to it with epoxy adhesive.

Before laying tile, sand off paint and dirt and roughen coating so that adhesive will adhere to the metal. On fireboxes, use heat-resistant epoxy thinset.

Wainscoting

Traditional wainscoting is made from tongue-and-groove boards; modern wainscoting from grooved plywood. Neither is an acceptable substrate for tile installation because they are not smooth enough to ensure good adhesion. Replace wainscoting with wallboard, plywood, or CBU.

Tiled wainscoting is acceptable as a tiling surface as long as it is in good condition.

Wallboard

Also known as gypsum board and drywall, and by various trade names, unpainted wallboard is an excellent substrate for tile.

New installations. Standard wallboard, which has a gray covering, is fine for use as a substrate in dry areas. But because it disintegrates when wet, it should not be used in areas that get wet, such as bathrooms. Instead, use water-resistant wallboard, recognizable by the blue or green covering.

Some tiled walls will look better if the tiles are set on a thick bed and edged with radius trim tiles. This look can be achieved by attaching two layers of wallboard to the area to be tiled. Install the second layer of wallboard by screwing or nailing the panels in place with fasteners long enough to penetrate through the first layer and into the studs.

Whether installing single or double layers of wallboard, leave a ⅛-inch gap between edges of sheets, cover the joint with fiberglass-mesh tape, and apply tile adhesive to seal the joint and reduce cracking. Cover nail heads and seal all edges with tape. Smooth away any excess adhesive and dust the surface with a damp rag before applying the tile adhesive.

Existing installations. Tile can be successfully installed over existing wallboard if it is clean, undamaged, and free of mildew. Remove any wallpaper and loosen paint from wallboard, then scrub surface with a strong cleanser. Sand any glossy surfaces and wipe with a damp cloth to remove dust. Repair holes or cracks with a wallboard patching compound before applying tile adhesive.

For dry installations, use a latex or acrylic thinset, a water-mixed thinset, or an organic mastic as the setting material. For wet installations, add a waterproofing membrane and use a latex or acrylic thinset adhesive.

Wallpaper

Wallpaper must be stripped before tiling. Once the wallpaper is removed, clean off any residual glue and wash the wall with a damp rag.

Install tile using a latex or water-mixed thinset or an organic mastic.

MEMBRANES

Various membranes can protect a tile installation from damage and deterioration. Not every installation needs these special treatments, and sometimes a membrane can perform more than one function.

Waterproofing Membrane

Glazed ceramic tiles will not be damaged by water, but the surface underneath them may be. A waterproofing membrane installed on the setting bed prevents moisture from penetrating into the substrate and causing serious problems.

Obviously, a waterproofing membrane is only necessary in wet installations, and the type used depends on whether the area will be merely exposed to water or will have water standing in it. Above the waterline, use a waterproof membrane that will protect construction. For installations below the waterline, you must install a tub or shower pan.

Among the all-purpose waterproofing systems available are sheet materials or single- or multicomponent liquid materials that are applied with a trowel. Some of these products double as reinforcing agents, adding tensile strength and preventing cracks. Application methods vary; check the label or ask for advice when purchasing the product.

Tar paper, layered with hot asphalt, is the traditional waterproofing membrane for use above a waterline. It is inexpensive, fairly durable, and easy to install. Nowadays, however, chlorinated polyethylene (CPE) is the most commonly used material and has proved to be more successful than "hot mopped" installations. CPE waterproofing membranes are flex-ible sheets that are available in 30-mil and 40-mil thicknesses. They come packaged in rolls 48, 60, and 72 inches wide. Check local building codes for the thickness demanded.

Installing a CPE Shower Pan

Before you start, make sure that the substrate slopes toward the drain and that it has nothing that could pierce the sheet. Sweep up any loose dirt and countersink any nail or screwheads. When using CPE membrane to waterproof a shower pan, use a bolt-down, clamping-ring type of drain with weepholes. Install it so the lip of the subdrain is flush with the substrate.

At the shower opening, continue CPE membrane up and over the curb (fastening it on the outside face of the curb) and extend it at least six inches beyond the curb of the pan. On enclosed walls, extend the membrane up and over the curb and at least one to three inches up the walls. Nail through the top edge only.

Carefully cut a hole the exact size of the drain opening. The membrane should fit tightly around any other plumbing: Instead of cutting holes, merely pierce the membrane and push plumbing through. Spread solvent cement between membrane and subdrain and bolt down clamping ring firmly. Place a small amount of gravel or other porous material at the weepholes so they will not get clogged by tile-setting materials.

If the membrane consists of more than one piece, overlap separate sheets by about two inches. Fold back the top edge and apply a solvent cement to both surfaces. Wait about two minutes then press edges together while cement is still tacky. Press lightly at first making sure the membrane is correctly positioned, then press firmly to weld the separate sheets together.

Before installing the tile, plug the subdrain and fill the pan with at least three inches of water. Let water stand for 24 hours so that you can make sure the clamping ring is tight and the pan is completely waterproof.

Isolation Membranes

An isolation membrane is placed on top of the setting bed to protect tile from the stress of seasonal swelling and contraction. Isolation membranes are especially important when tile is installed on a concrete slab, or when the bed is composed of two different materials (for instance, a bed that is half plywood and half concrete slab).

If the existing setting bed is structurally sound, an isolation membrane is probably not necessary. If the structure has visible cracks, installing such a membrane may be advisable. A pliable CPE and polyester-fiber sheet product is a suitable product for most residential installations.

Curing Membranes

A curing membrane is only necessary for cement-mortar tile installations, which are best left to professionals. It is placed between the setting bed and the framing to prevent water from evaporating too quickly. Tar paper is the best material to use for this function.

First spread roofing asphalt over the underlayment, embed and nail tar paper in place, then float the mortar bed on top of the paper. Set tile on adhesive over the mortar bed. After the installation has hardened, the curing bed will also function as an isolation membrane.

Important: Be sure that any materials used for waterproofing are compatible with the setting materials you will be using.

THINSET

Setting materials are the adhesives that hold tile to the substrate. Adhesive must be compatible with the substrate to ensure a good bond—this is the key to an installation that will last.

Before selecting an adhesive, determine the type of substrate you will be tiling over. Next, consider whether or not the site is exposed to water. With these factors in mind, you can make a choice depending on the cost of the adhesive, ease of installation, and availability.

There are several types and countless brands of adhesives, and new setting materials are constantly being developed. Salespeople can provide information on various brands. Look for the Tile Council of America or the Ceramic Tile Institute seal on product labels. These organizations test products before issuing their approval.

Installation

In the past few decades new types of tile adhesives have been developed, revolutionizing tile installation and making it accessible to the layperson. Most of the new products are called thinset adhesives, and the process of using them to install tile is called thinsetting or a thin-bed installation.

Modern thinset adhesives are perfectly suitable for most residential tile projects, and all tile-installation procedures in this book refer to the thinsetting method.

Thinset installation refers to the process of installing tiles on a bed so that the tiles adhere not to each other but to the substrate below. The "thin" reflects the fact that the bonding material is usually only ⅛ to ¼ inch thick.

Thinset installation is fairly easy to master. With a little practice, anyone can install ceramic tile, stone products, and pavers using the thinset-installation method. Except when the substrate needs truing or leveling with thick-bed mortar, thinset-tile installation is suitable for all residential sites. Step-by-step thinset-installation guidelines begin on page 65.

The term thinset is also used generically to describe several of the materials used in the method. Organic mastic, another type of adhesive, is also applied using thinset installation techniques.

Organic Mastic

Organic mastic is a material for bonding tile that cures by evaporation. This type of adhesive is suitable for installing ceramic tile on interior floors, walls, and countertops.

Organic mastics are purchased premixed; no further addition of liquid or powder is necessary. There are two basic types of organic mastic. Latex-based mastics contain water; petrochemical-based mastics contain a solvent called toluene. Each type is made up of two components: a bonding agent and a mixing agent.

Do not use a petrochemical-based mastic to set finished marble; the chemicals will discolor the stone. Latex-based organic mastics and any of the thinset adhesives can be used with stone tile products.

Because organic mastics are premixed, they are the easiest and most commonly used adhesives for residential use. They are especially popular for use on walls because they hold tiles as soon as they are set in place, eliminating tile slippage.

Mastics can be used in dry installations with plywood, wallboard, plaster, portland-cement mortar, formed concrete, and masonry substrates. Not all mastics are compatible with all substrates so check product labels.

Organic mastics can be used in properly prepared wet areas, though considerable care should be taken if applying a mastic in a heavily used wet area. Suitable substrates in wet areas include plywood, portland-cement mortar, formed concrete, masonry, and GMMU backer board (however, some types of GMMU should not be used on floors; follow manufacturer's recommendations).

Organic mastics are not suitable for use around swimming pools or in exterior installations, nor should they be used in areas exposed to heat, such as fireplace surrounds and hearths. Check product labels for appropriate uses of individual brands.

Despite their ease of use and popularity, organic mastics are inferior to thinset adhesives in a number of ways. They do not have the bond strength, bond flexibility, or comprehensive strength of thinset adhesives, although the bond strength of organic mastics varies greatly between brands. Organic mastics are slightly less expensive than water-mixed, latex, and acrylic thinsets.

Use caution when working with organic mastics. The vapors in petrochemical-based mastics are flammable and dangerous when inhaled. Wear a charcoal-filter dust mask at all times. Do not smoke while working with these adhesives. Extinguish any open flames—even pilot lights—near the work area. Latex-based mastics are not quite as dangerous as the petrochemical-based varieties, but it is wise to observe these safety precautions rather than risking serious injury.

Mastics are sold in cans. There may be some oil or water floating on the surface when the can is opened. Thoroughly mix the ingredients before use. If the mastic is difficult to stir, it may be too old to use and should be returned.

You can store leftover organic mastic in a cool, dark place but it does not keep very well, even in a properly sealed can, so try to purchase only the amount needed.

Tile-installation procedures are basically the same whether you are using an organic mastic or a thinset adhesive. The substrate should be prepared according to the mastic manufacturer's directions. Surfaces must be absolutely flat, much more so than for thinset adhesives. Organic mastic cannot be used to fill in low spots in the substrate because the thicker areas may not dry thoroughly enough to reach maximum bond strength. Apply organic mastic using the method outlined on page 65.

Product labels indicate open time (the amount of time the spread adhesive can be exposed to air before tiles are set into it) and curing time (the time the adhesive must cure before grouting can take place).

Clean tools and mastic spills as soon as possible, while the mastic is still soft. Hardened mastic is nearly impossible to get off. Remove solvent-based mastic with paint thinner; for water-based mastic, use water.

Thinset Adhesives

Several different adhesives fall into this category. All thinset adhesives are powdered sand-and-portland-cement products that must be mixed before use. The three types most often used in residential installations are water-mixed thinset, latex and acrylic thinsets, and epoxy thinset.

Thinset adhesives have greater bond strength, greater compressive strength, and more flexibility than organic mastics. Because thinsets can support more weight, they are preferred for floor installations. Thinset adhesives cure more quickly than mastics and can be used for both dry and wet installations and near heat.

Thinset adhesives are generally more expensive than organic mastics. Water-mixed, latex, and acrylic thinsets are about equal in price, and are considerably less expensive than epoxy thinsets.

Water-mixed thinset. Also called dry-set mortar, water-mixed thinset is a mixture of portland cement, sand, and additives that slow the curing process. Water-mixed thinset is suitable for use in both dry and wet installations, inside and outside.

Once cured, water-based thinset is not affected by prolonged contact with water, but does not form a water barrier. It is not intended for leveling or truing the substrate. Suitable substrates for use with this type of adhesive include properly prepared masonry, concrete, plywood, GMMU, cured cement-mortar beds, brick, ceramic tile, and dimensioned stone. Product labels describe specific uses.

Water-mixed thinset is not flammable and gives off no fumes, but the mixture can be irritating to skin and breathing passages. Wear a charcoal-filter dust mask and rubber gloves when mixing and applying thinsets.

While soft, water-mixed thinset can be cleaned with water. Once cured, it is difficult to remove from tools, tiles, and body parts. Do not attempt to store mixed thinset. Product labels indicate curing times.

Latex and acrylic thinsets. These thinsets consist of a combination of portland cement, sand, and either latex (natural rubber) or acrylic (synthetic rubber) additives. Latex and acrylic thinsets have greater bond strength, higher compressive strength, and more flexibility than water-mixed thinsets.

Most latex and acrylic thinsets can be used over any backing material, although some are not recommended for use over plywood. Latex and acrylic thinsets are highly water resistant, though not waterproof. With a proper waterproofing membrane, they can be used in wet installations.

The dry components of latex and acrylic thinsets are purchased in sacks, and the liquid additives in separate jars.

Although the materials are not flammable or dangerous, the dust that rises when the adhesives are mixed can be annoying. Wear a charcoal-filter dust mask and rubber gloves when working with latex and acrylic thinsets.

Spilled latex and acrylic thinset must be cleaned immediately with a sponge and water. If allowed to harden, this type of adhesive is very difficult to remove from skin, tools, and tile.

Epoxy thinset. Epoxy adhesives are made up of a combination of liquid resin, liquid hardener, and a sand-and-cement mixture designed for use on floors, walls, and countertops. They have high bond and compressive strength and are flexible after curing. Epoxy thinsets cure quickly and are fairly easy to apply, making them ideal for use on surfaces that must be returned to service as soon as possible. Their chemical and solvent resistance tends to be better than that of organic mastic.

Epoxy thinsets should not be confused with all-purpose epoxy used for household repairs. Epoxy thinsets are specifically for use with tile.

Epoxy thinsets can be used on any substrate. They are water-resistant and can be used in wet installations if the surface is prepared with a waterproofing membrane; they are also suitable for dry installations.

Although epoxy thinsets are more expensive than other adhesives, they should be used when tiling over a substrate that is incompatible with other adhesives or when there is any doubt about the bonding capabilities needed for a particular type of tile.

Epoxy materials are not especially dangerous, but dust and vapors can be irritating to skin and breathing passages, so take safety precautions. Wear a charcoal-filter dust mask and rubber gloves while mixing and working with epoxy thinsets.

Clean tools, tiles, and spills before the epoxy thinset hardens. Some brands are water soluble; others require a solvent cleaner. Check product labels for specific directions.

GROUT

Grout is the material placed between tiles once they are bonded to the substrate. It fills the joints, protects the edges, prevents water and moisture from coming into contact with the adhesive, and adds the finishing touch to all tile jobs.

Most grout comes in powdered form and is mixed with water or with latex or acrylic additives in ratios listed on the product label. Some new cement-grout products are available in cartridges similar to those used for applying caulk. These products should be applied according to the manufacturer's directions. Instructions for applying traditional grout can be found on page 77.

If installing pregrouted ceramic-tile sheets, use the same type of grout between sheets as was used between the tiles, or a type recommended by the manufacturer.

Portland-cement Grout

Plain portland-cement grout produces a water-resistant, dense, uniformly colored grout joint. The variety used on walls is usually white and contains very fine aggregate, making it slightly rough. Grout for floors is usually gray and is designed for use with ceramic mosaic, quarry, and paver tiles.

Use this type of grout for joints less than 1/8 inch wide. Some brands are designed for use with a specific type of tile, others can be used with any kind of tile.

After grouting with plain portland cement, occasionally mist the installation with water for the next couple of days. This will slow down the curing and strengthen the grout.

Sanded Portland-cement Grout

This type of grout is plain portland-cement grout with sand added for increased strength. Use sanded grout for joints wider than 1/16 inch. Sanded portland-cement grout is used with ceramic mosaic, quarry, and paver tiles on floors and walls.

As with with plain portland cement, keep misting the installation with water for 24 hours to slow down the curing.

Dry-set Grout

This type of grout is a mixture of portland cement and additives that provide water retention. It is suitable for grouting all tiles subject to ordinary use in any location.

Although misting newly grouted joints may help develop greater strength, it is not absolutely required when grouting with dry-set grout.

Latex and Acrylic Additives

The use of a latex or acrylic grout additive is highly recommended for all interior tile installations. Latex (natural rubber) and acrylic (synthetic rubber) additives give grout added properties such as color retention, mildew resistance, flexibility, freeze-thaw stability, uniformity, spreadability, slower curing time, hardness, stain resistance, strength, and water resistance. Most importantly, these additives eliminate the need for damp curing the grout.

Although these additives are very helpful, they can also cause some problems. They will carry the pigment of the grout into the tile, so unglazed tiles must be sealed before grouting. Additives will also make their way into any cracks in the glaze of a glazed tile. If using additives in the grout, test one tile from each box to make sure that the grout can be removed from the tile face.

Additives can be mixed into any of the three types of grout that are described above prior to application. Product labels list ratios and specific directions.

Colored Grout

With the enormous range of colors available, it is highly unlikely that you will not be able to obtain the exact shade you require. But should this happen, many tile stores can customize grout color in much the same way that paint stores can mix up paint to match a color chip.

Do not judge color by the dry powder. Generally, tile suppliers have cured samples of the colored grouts they stock. These are often in the form of narrow "sticks" that simulate a joint. If you place these sticks between two of your chosen tiles, you will be able to imagine what the completed installation will look like.

CAULK & SEALER

Water seeping through a tile installation will ruin the substrate. Also, if the problem is not corrected, it will cause structural members to rot.

Although grout protects the substrate from water damage, it is not waterproof. In areas that will be constantly exposed to water, you should seal joints, caulk them, or do both.

Caulk

Silicone caulk is a soft, puttylike, waterproof sealer that should be used around sinks and plumbing fixtures, and in expansion joints on both indoor and outdoor installations. (An expansion joint is the space left between two materials that will not expand and contract at the same rate.)

Caulk does not require any mixing. It is furnished in prepackaged tubes or cartridges in a limited range of colors. It should be applied according to manufacturer's directions after grout has cured completely.

Sealers

Sealers can be used on virtually all unglazed tile and stone products, both inside and outside.

Stain prevention is the main reason to seal a tile installation. Almost any porous tile will stain; light-colored tiles stain especially easily.

In most cases a sealed tile can be cleaned by simple damp mopping or, on outdoor installations, a hosing. However, depending on the type of sealer used, it may be necessary to wax in order to protect the sealer and maintain the glossy finish.

Enhancing or changing the appearance of the tile is another reason for applying a sealer. Use a glossy sealer to bring out the natural texture and color variation of a rustic paver.

Sealers may also be used to darken or lighten a porous paver.

Types of Sealers

There are two basic types of sealers: water-based and oil-based. Oil-based sealers repel both water-based and oil-based liquids. Both types of sealers must be removed with solvent, lacquer thinner, acetone, or paint stripper. Sealers are available in two general categories: penetrating sealers and coating sealers. The former are designed to be absorbed into the surface of tiles and grout, and usually do not leave a sheen on the surface after they are applied. Their primary function is to reduce the absorbancy of the tile surface. Some types of penetrating sealers, particularly oil-based sealers, may make the surface slightly darker in appearance.

Coating sealers are designed to remain on the surface of the tile, and generally leave a sheen or gloss. Like penetrating sealers, their primary function is to reduce the absorbancy of the tile and grout. Tile finished with a coating sealer often requires waxing to protect the sealer.

Lacquer-based sealers penetrate unglazed tile pores, making the tiles water-resistant and protecting them from moisture and stains. These products are available in both gloss and matte finishes. (Some gloss finishes can be slippery when wet, so test before applying on floors.)

Grout sealers. Use a grout sealer in all wet installations. Silicone-based sealers should be used to seal grout around tubs and other areas that get wet, but should not be used on surfaces where food will be prepared.

Check that the sealer you purchase is recommended for the type of grout you are using and make sure it can be used over colored grout if that is what will be used.

Natural sealer. Use natural lemon oil to seal grout on countertops around food-preparation areas. Lemon oil is not expensive and can be purchased at a grocery store.

Applying a sealer brings out the depth and luster of slate tiles. Dark grout deemphasizes the joints, thereby accentuating the tiles rather than the grid.

INSTALLING TILE

There is nothing particularly difficult about installing tile. In fact, the main requirement is patience. That, along with a good eye for detail, is the only talent needed to correctly set tile.

The tile itself is a finishing material, the most visible part of the installation. The materials underneath and the way they are installed are equally important. Tile must be laid out correctly, set onto correctly spread adhesive, and placed on a solid substrate. The finishing touches to a tile job—grouting, sealing, and cleanup—ensure its beauty and durability.

Understanding the right way to install tile will ensure a high-quality job that you can be proud of and that will serve you well for years to come.

An important characteristic of a professional-looking tile installation is consistently straight and uniform grout joints. Plastic spacers make this easy to achieve.

PREPARING TO TILE

Installing tile will disrupt your life-style, no matter how small the installation. To minimize the inconvenience, be sure to have all tools and setting materials on hand, tile selected, and design planned before beginning any tile installation.

If you are installing tile in the midst of other construction, be sure to consult with members of the construction crew regarding the suitable timing of the tile installation, and to caution them as to the location of newly installed tile.

A large part of preparing to tile is planning the schedule. Determine how long the total tile installation will take and identify alternatives for the kitchen, bath, or other room that will be out of commission. In addition to the time needed for the preparation, layout, and tile-installation steps (which depends on the size of the job), add at least 24 hours for the adhesive to cure and another 24 hours for the grout to set. If the tile must be sealed, add another day for the sealer to dry. You'll be able to use the room after that; however, the tile will not be fully cured until about a month after installation, and any newly tiled surface should be treated carefully during the curing period.

Obviously, you will need to remove all furniture and movable objects from the room to be tiled. Take the time to protect all surrounding areas. Use tape to cover edges of wallpapered or painted walls that abut areas to be tiled. Mask the lower edges of finished walls where they meet a floor that will be tiled. Use drafting tape rather than standard masking tape on wallpapered surfaces; the adhesive on drafting tape is less likely to mar the wallcovering.

Use paper or plastic to protect cabinets and sinks that will be left in place. Spread drop cloths over tubs and any appliances left in the room. Be sure to cover drain holes and any exposed pipes to prevent tile adhesive and grout from clogging them.

Before Tiling Floors

Make sure the floor surface to be tiled is sound, smooth, and clean. The exact surface preparation will depend on whether you are using an existing or a new substrate. See Suitable Substrates, page 38, to determine what kind of preparation your floor requires.

In general, repair any cracks in the flooring and remove any waxes, finishes, and dirt from existing surfaces. Vacuum dust from all surrounding surfaces after making any of the preparations listed below, and perhaps again after the layout step to ensure that the adhesive is applied to as clean a surface as possible.

Plan new traffic patterns while the floor is curing or prepare some plywood squares that can be placed on top of newly set tiles and used as stepping stones. Walk cautiously and check tile alignment if you feel any movement as you step on the floor.

Doors

Because the tile will raise the height of the floor, you will probably need to trim the lower edges of all doors in the room. Interior doors require a ¼-inch clearance; exterior doors should be measured to determine necessary clearance (remember to take the height of weather stripping into account).

If a door needs trimming, remove it prior to installing tile. Remove doors by tapping out hinge pins. After the tile job is finished, measure distance from bottom of lower hinge on door jamb to top of the floor tile, subtract ¼ inch, mark that distance from corresponding point on door, and cut door to new length.

Baseboards

You may decide to install new baseboard to coordinate with the tile. Tile, wood, vinyl, and plastic baseboards are available. No matter which type you select, installing a baseboard over a completed tile installation looks and functions better than butting tile to an existing one; the baseboard hides rough edges of tiles. When remodeling, remove the existing baseboard during the preparation stage.

Remove a baseboard by first removing the finishing nails. Either pry them away from the wall using a pry bar, or hammer them completely through the board and into the wall using a hammer and an awl. Then lift the baseboard away. If you intend to reinstall the same baseboard, use caution during removal and mark each piece to ensure that it is returned to the correct position.

In some older homes the baseboard is finished with a strip of shoe molding, a rounded strip that sits directly on the floor. If that is the case, remove only the shoe molding and leave the baseboard in place. The edge of the tile will be covered when the shoe molding is replaced.

Thresholds

A threshold is the transition piece between two floors of differing heights or materials. Most common thresholds are made of a hardwood such as oak, cut and finished marble, or aluminum. Wood and metal thresholds are installed with screws sunk into the substrate; marble thresholds are attached with tile adhesive. In new installations, leave a space and install the threshold after the tile installation is completed.

If you choose to retain an existing threshold, leave a ⅛-inch gap between the last row of tiles and the threshold, and fill this joint with silicone caulk. If you intend to install a new threshold, remove and discard the existing threshold during the preparation stage.

Be aware of thresholds during layout, and try not to position small cut tiles directly in front of them. Make sure that flooring from one room is not visible in the adjoining room when the door is closed. A wider threshold should solve this problem if it arises.

Toilets
If you are tiling around an existing toilet, install tiles to within ⅛ inch of the fixture and finish the joint with silicone caulk.

If you are tiling a new bathroom and the toilet has not yet been installed, you may prefer to set tiles before you put in the toilet. This allows you to hide cut tiles under the fixture and makes a neater edge.

Pedestals and Wall-mounted Sinks
All pedestals, wall-mounted sinks with support legs, and vanities should be removed before tiling the floor or wall. Follow the same basic steps to remove any of these. First, turn off water at shutoff valve under sink. Disconnect supply lines. Remove trap from sink using a pipe wrench. Unbolt connecting nuts from wall and floor and rock sink to break the seal. Lift sink off the floor and from brackets attached to the wall.

Before removing sink completely, test that finished height of newly tiled floor (and thickness of wall, if you are tiling that as well) will not make it impossible to reconnect pipes and brackets. Put a piece of wood or other material that is as thick as your tile under the pedestal, and check that pipe and bracket fittings will align. Most supply pipes have enough give or can be bent enough to accommodate new floor or wall thickness. However, you may need to

purchase pipe extenders. Some wall brackets are designed to sit on top of finished tile. You may need to purchase new brackets and install them on top of the finished tiles to compensate for the new height of the floor and thickness of the wall.

Floor Pipes
Mask around and over all pipes for sinks, toilets, heating elements, radiators, and hot water delivery, as well as vacuum attachment receptacles. Although tile adhesives shouldn't splash, any adhesive that found its way into these openings would be difficult to remove. Set tiles to within ⅛ inch of these fittings and fill the joint with silicone caulk, which will allow pipes to move slightly as they expand and contract.

Before Tiling Walls
The specific preparation required for a wall depends on the type of substrate selected (see page 38). On existing walls remove all fixtures, such as towel bars and switch plates, and fill holes as needed. Use a heavy-duty household cleanser to remove all grease and dirt, which can affect the bonding capability of the adhesive.

Window and Door Casings
These can be either retained or removed, depending on your design. If retained, set tile to within ¼ inch of casing and fill the joint with grout. If you prefer to have the casing over the tile to cover cut tile edges, remove casing during the preparation stage and clean away any debris and dust from behind it. When reinstalling, cut a groove in the back of the casing to accommodate the thickness of the tile.

Electrical Outlets
Outlet boxes must be flush with the finished surface of a tiled wall or floor. If you are installing tile on an existing wall with an electrical outlet, you must adjust the utility boxes during the preparation stage.

To adjust a box, shut off power to the outlet. Remove switch plate and screws holding box to wall. If your tile is ⅜ inch thick or less, you can simply reposition the box. Pull box forward enough so that it will be flush with surface of tile. If your tile is thicker than ⅜ inch, you will probably need to purchase a box extender and install it according to the manufacturer's directions prior to installing tile.

If your design calls for changing the location of an electrical outlet, consult an electrical repair book or hire a licensed contractor to do the work before you begin the tiling job.

Shower and Tub Fixtures
Unless you are installing new substrate, fixtures do not need to be removed before tiling a wall. Just be sure that they are well masked and loosen the escutcheons. Set tiles within ¼ inch of each fixture and fill the joint with silicone caulk.

If you are installing new substrate or replacing the shower and tub fixtures, you'll need to remove the shower head, tub spout, and faucet assemblies. Turn off water supply, remove fixtures, and mask them well. An inexpensive and easy way to protect pipes is to screw on pipe nipples (short lengths of pipe that are threaded on one end and capped on the other).

Set tiles within ¼ inch of pipes. After tiles have been grouted, replace pipe nipple with shower head, tub spout, or faucet assembly. Fill joint between tile and fixture with silicone caulk.

The change in thickness of a wall is usually not a problem when replacing faucet assemblies; simply turn the fixtures fewer times than before to tighten.

Wall Pipes
All water and vacuum attachment pipes should be masked before tiling; see Floor Pipes, above.

Before Tiling Countertops

Check that the countertop assembly is sound. Be sure that the surface is level, smooth, and square. Identify any problem areas and repair as needed. Specific countertop preparations depend on the type of substrate used (see page 38).

As long as you are capable of disconnecting and reattaching supply lines, most countertop installations can be accomplished without having to hire a plumber. However, if the sink or faucets need to be moved more than a couple of inches, professional help may be necessary.

Sinks

Recessed, surface-mounted, or self-rimming sinks can be accommodated in a tiled countertop but an existing sink must be removed for a neat and watertight installation. Always shut off the water supply before doing anything else.

Detach faucets and control valves keeping track of all parts. Check that all of the attachments will fit through any new backing materials and tile; adding pipe extenders may be necessary. Lengthening pipe an inch or two is not difficult.

To remove a recessed sink, unscrew clamps on underside of sink and lower it away from countertop. You may have to pry away any caulk or edging materials that finish the rim on top side of countertop.

To remove a surface-mounted or self-rimming sink, unscrew clamps on underside of sink, use a putty knife to loosen sealant around rim, and lift sink away from countertop.

If you plan to relocate the sink within the new tiled countertop, you will need to do some plumbing work or call in professional help.

Appliances

Move appliances out of a room prior to tiling a floor or wall, and always install tiles under and behind appliance locations. Although you may think this flooring will never be ex-posed, you can never be sure of future remodeling needs.

Also, if you only tile up to the front of an undercounter appliance, it will be trapped in position and either the tile or the counter will have to be demolished in order to replace the appliance.

Before moving appliances, check their heights in conjunction with new floor and countertop heights. Make sure that after the height of the floor or the thickness of countertop edging is changed, the doors of the dishwasher, clothes dryer, trash compactor, and other appliances will clear the edge of the countertop, and the stove and refrigerator will fit underneath overhead cabinets.

If a door will not clear, you must raise the height of the countertop or replace or trim the cabinet.

Faucet Assembly

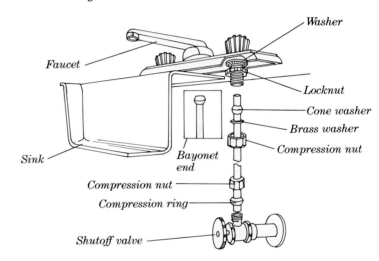

Washer
Faucet
Locknut
Cone washer
Brass washer
Compression nut
Sink
Bayonet end
Compression nut
Compression ring
Shutoff valve

Waste Pipe Assembly

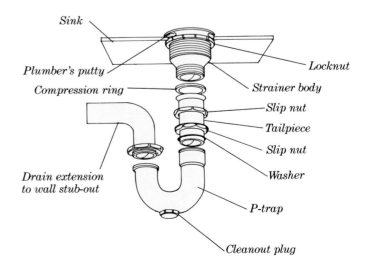

Sink
Plumber's putty
Locknut
Strainer body
Compression ring
Slip nut
Tailpiece
Slip nut
Washer
Drain extension to wall stub-out
P-trap
Cleanout plug

Several tile makers and wallcovering manufacturers have joined forces to produce matching lines. If these don't suit, you can commission an artist to paint and fire accent tiles especially for you. Or you can make your own: Tile blanks, special paints, and instructions are available at many craft stores.

LAYOUT TOOLS

Most of the tools needed for laying out a tile installation are items that you should either have or be able to borrow for the short time you'll need them. The most important layout tool is a jury stick, and that's something you must make for each job.

What You'll Need

Be sure to check the accuracy of all your layout tools before you use them; a crooked straightedge will do you no good at all.

Drawing Tools

To make a plan view drawing and to sketch a tile layout on paper, you'll find ⅛-inch or ¼-inch graph paper handy, as well as a standard ruler, a pencil, and an eraser.

Squaring Tools

To check for level and square, you'll need a spirit level and a framing square. An accurate tape measure and a couple of straightedges (one short and one medium length) are necessary for drawing reference lines. The straightedges, level, and square will also be used for tile alignment during tile setting.

Plumb Bob

A plumb bob is a small weight attached to the end of a string. If you don't own one and don't wish to buy one, you can make your own by attaching to a string anything heavy enough to pull the string tight. Hang the weighted string from a nail tacked to the wall and, when it stops swinging, you will have a true vertical reference line. Use a square to establish a true horizontal line.

Chalk Line

To mark reference lines for a small installation, you can use straightedges and a pencil or piece of chalk, but for large areas a chalk line is much more accurate. This tool is merely a length of string housed in a dispenser that contains chalk. Unreel the string, hold it taut, and snap it to leave a chalked line on the setting surface.

Jury Stick

A jury stick, also called a story pole or a tile-setting stick, is a homemade ruler marked with tile and joint widths rather than inches and feet. This simple measuring instrument costs practically nothing to make and is an invaluable layout aid. It allows you to lay out your tile installation without having to calculate each dimension or without setting each tile down in place.

To make a jury stick, use any piece of straight wood about 8 to 10 feet long. (A length of pine lattice board is light, inexpensive, and easy to handle.) You may need more than one jury stick if you are tiling a floor with short and long dimensions or if you are using tiles of more than one size.

Starting at one end of the stick, make appropriate marks to indicate the grout-joint width. Next to that, mark the width of a tile. Repeat joint/tile/joint/tile measurements along the length of the stick. If the tiles you are using vary in size (handmade tiles and pavers can vary by as much as ½ inch), use an average tile width to mark the increments on the jury stick.

Making a Jury Stick

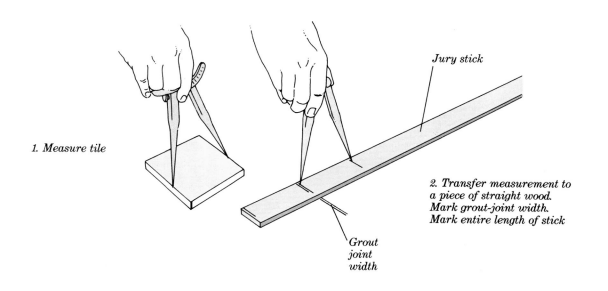

1. Measure tile

Jury stick

2. Transfer measurement to a piece of straight wood. Mark grout-joint width. Mark entire length of stick

Grout joint width

LAYOUT PRINCIPLES

Layout is a preliminary step in tile setting that allows you to visualize an installation before you even open a can of adhesive.

Although many experienced tile setters will install tile without first determining the layout, this shortcut is not recommended. The benefits of performing the layout step include being able to:
□ Decide on the best arrangement of the entire field of tiles.
□ Experiment with the placement of specialty or feature tiles.
□ Arrange tiles so that cut edges will be least noticeable.
□ Ascertain how much cutting you will have to do.
□ Make an accurate tile and materials estimate, thereby avoiding last-minute surprises that mean another trip to the store.

Discover problems, such as rooms out of square, early enough to adjust for them.

Rarely does a tile layout work out in such a way that the entire job can be done with full tiles. Almost all tile projects require cutting some tiles to fit along edges, around fixtures, and the like, but the fewer cut tiles there are, the better an installation will look. Therefore, the two overriding principles of layout are to use as many full tiles as possible, and to place the cut ones where they will be least noticeable.

Layout Procedure

Whether you are laying out a floor, wall, or countertop, the steps are basically the same:
1. Determine focal point or points.
2. Establish reference lines.
3. Test various layouts using a jury stick or actual tiles with spacers between them.
4. Adjust reference lines as needed

to create the best-looking installation with the least number of cut tiles.

Finding a good layout requires exploring various possibilities and then deciding on the solution that pleases you most.

Determining Focal Points

Before beginning the layout, spend some time looking at the surface or surfaces to be tiled and identifying the focal points, or most noticeable areas in a room.

The most visible parts of a wall installation are generally the areas directly opposite the doorway and just above a sink or tub. For floor installations, check where you look when you first enter the room, and take note of other thresholds, the area in front of a fireplace or television, centers of furniture groupings, and counters or built-ins that divide the

space. On countertops, the spots flanking a sink or cooktop will be most noticed and most used, as will the center section of a bar top. On island counters, the corners and edges will be very visible.

Design your layout using parallel lines and full tiles at these focal points. Generally, the most attractive layout is one in which the cut tiles are symmetrical; that is, cut tiles of equal size are placed on both sides of a field of full tiles. Whenever possible, cut edges should be placed where they will be hidden from view under baseboards, moldings, cabinets, trim tiles, or backsplashes.

About Square

Almost all rooms are out of square; that is, not all of the walls meet each other and the floor at exact 90-degree angles, and therefore opposing walls are not exactly parallel. This

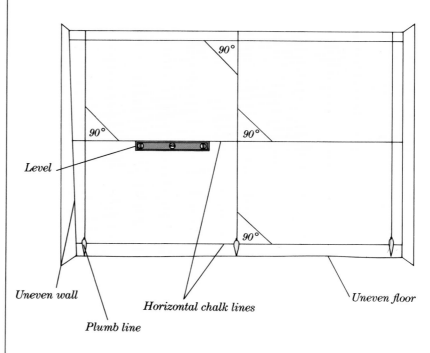

Reference Lines for Wall Installation

Establishing Square

To check that reference lines are exactly perpendicular, measure out 3' from the corner in one direction and 4' in the other. Diagonal line joining the 2 points should measure 5'. This formula works using any multiple of 3:4:5. For example, 6:8:10 or 4½:6:7½

Fill with cut tiles

L-Shape

Start installation here to ensure full tiles where rows turn a corner

Fill with cut tiles

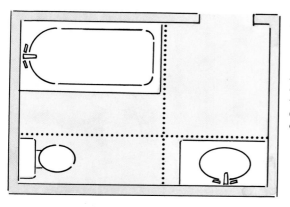

Focal Points

Reference lines should be parallel to most noticeable straight lines and perpendicular to each other

poses a problem when tiling: Because tiles are by nature exactly square (or rectangular), when they are installed on a surface that is not square, the faulty alignment becomes obvious. It is very important that you do not begin tiling at one corner and work across the area, since the resulting installation is likely to be completely misaligned. Instead, do a layout to determine where to begin tiling in order to avoid, or at least minimize, this problem.

Establishing Reference Lines

Establishing accurate starting or reference lines is crucial to the success of any tile project. These two lines, which are drawn to intersect at an angle of exactly 90 degrees, indicate the position of the first tile set; that first tile, in turn, determines the positioning and alignment of the entire installation.

If you are careful or if the area to be tiled is small, you can use a straightedge to draw the reference lines; if you do so, measure carefully to make sure they are straight. A more accurate method, especially on a large area, is to snap chalk lines (see page 52).

The following sections on walls, floors, and countertops describe how to plot reference lines.

On Walls
Plot reference lines using a plumb bob, a spirit level, and a framing square. Drop plumb bob at the exact center of the wall and mark this vertical reference line with a pencil or a chalk line. Make a horizontal reference line at about eye level, making sure it is exactly perpendicular to the vertical line.

Multiple walls. Extend horizontal reference line onto any other wall to be tiled so that grout joints will match.

On Floors
The procedure for marking reference lines on floors is similar to that for

walls, but varies somewhat depending on your particular floor plan.

Basically square floor. Plot reference lines that intersect at the exact center of the room or at a desired focal point.

L-shaped floor. Start as shown in the illustration on page 54 to ensure full tiles where rows turn the corner.

Built-ins. If the room to be tiled contains a built-in counter or a bar set at a right angle to the wall and the room is not square, you will have to make a decision. If you square the layout to the room, the built-in may appear crooked; if you square the layout to the built-in, the out-of-squareness may be emphasized. Try laying it out both ways then decide which looks best.

Multiple rooms. Draw initial reference line through the centerpoint of the doorway that connects the rooms to be tiled.

On Countertops

Because countertops are generally small enough to do a complete layout with dry tiles, you can draw the reference lines after you have tested various layouts.

Testing Layouts

Once you have drawn reference lines, the next step is to try various layouts to see how tiles will fall at ends of rows and around fixtures and other obstacles. If you are laying out a wall, you will need to use a jury stick for this step. If you are laying out a floor you will only be able to lay out a couple of rows. Use a jury stick to verify your placement. Layouts for walls or any other vertical surface will have to be determined with a jury stick. However, countertops and similar projects are small enough that you can probably do a complete layout with dry tiles. Even though you can use measuring tools to determine where cut tiles will be needed, actually putting a row of tiles in place and seeing what will happen at the end of the row makes it much easier to decide on adjustments. In order to

experiment with layouts, you will need to purchase some field tiles, a few trim tiles, and tile spacers.

When adjusting the layout, plan so that cut tiles end up in the least noticeable locations. Where cuts are necessary, avoid using pieces less than one third the size of a full tile; small pieces are more noticeable and are difficult to cut, place, and set.

Decide on the positions of specialty tiles at this time, too. Attach cove and trim tiles temporarily to setting surface with masking tape while considering their placement.

Making Adjustments

Layout is a process of experimentation. If you end up with a small space to fill or with a layout that requires cut tiles in noticeable places, there are three simple ways to make adjustments. You may come up with others.
1. Shift all the tiles a few inches one way or another. This requires erasing the reference line, but it is well worth the extra time. These adjustments make the difference between a professional-looking installation and a sloppy one.

Adjusting Cut Tile Dimension

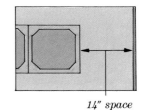
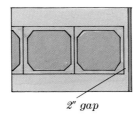

2" gap   *14" space*

1. Tiles are 12" square and there is a 2" gap at end of row

2. Remove last tile and divide new space (14") in half (7")

3. Adjust row accordingly

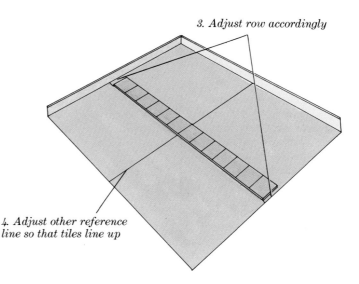

4. Adjust other reference line so that tiles line up

2. Adjust the width of the grout joints. Generally it will be necessary to re-adjust the grout lines over the entire layout, although there may be cases in which a difference in one area will not be noticeable.

3. Consider adding different-size tiles as a border or to define a particular area. Obviously this will greatly affect the look of the layout, but—if well planned—it can make the overall design more interesting.

Adjusting Wall Layout

Decide whether you prefer to have cut tiles along the top or the base of the wall. The least noticeable location is usually the best choice; remember also that you can hide cut tiles at the top or base of a wall with molding or a baseboard.

If cut tiles will be at wall base, measure down from the ceiling at several points, marking the width of one full tile plus a grout joint. Join up these points; the resulting line will indicate the lower edge of a theoretical final row. Measure the distance between this line and the horizontal reference line at several points. If distances are equal, you are in luck: You can plan the layout with a full tile at the ceiling edge. If distances are not equal (which means the wall is not square to the ceiling), there are several possible solutions, which are described below. If your aim is to have full tiles at the floor edge, use the same procedure but draw the line indicating the final row at the lower edge of the wall.

Next check the horizontal placement of tiles. Mark your jury stick, indicating the dimensions of both the tile and the grout joint. Move the stick along the horizontal reference line to find out how wide the last tile at each end of the row will be. If the last tiles will have to be cut down to less than one-third the width of a full tile, adjust and redraw the vertical reference line until the result is more pleasing.

If you will be using cove, bullnose, or other trim tiles, or will need to cut tiles to fit around fixtures, remember to take these into account when checking the layout.

Interruptions. If the wall is intersected by a counter, bathtub, window, or other focal point, you will have to decide whether it is more important to have full tiles at the ceiling edge or at the intersection of the wall and the interruption.

Generally, an installation will look better if there are full tiles along the edge of the tub or other interruption; in a bathroom or kitchen, this will also give you the advantage of a clean edge to caulk. But if the edge of a tub or counter is not level (not parallel to the horizontal reference line), you will be forced to taper-cut tiles to fit along the edge.

Corners. Use cove tiles or other corner trim pieces to round corners. These can be taped in place during layout. If corner pieces are not available to match the tile you have chosen, the neatest way to round an inside corner is to run tile on one wall right to the edge, and then cover the cut edge by starting with a full tile on the adjacent wall.

An outside corner looks best when the edge of a full tile on one wall is lapped by a full bullnose tile on the other wall. If this won't work, consider a piece of trim that will conceal cut edges.

Partial coverage. If the tile installation will stop in the middle of a wall (a tub surround, for example), you will need to trim the edge. A bullnose tile is the best thing to use in this case.

Bear in mind that this sort of installation will look much better if there is dimension to the tiled area; that is, if it is raised from the wall. If you are

using a thin tile, build up the substrate and trim the edge with a line of rounded grout or a row of edge tiles.

Problems with square. If a wall is only slightly out of square (a difference of 1/8 inch over a span of 8 feet, for example), adjust for the difference by simply varying the width of the last grout joint at the top, base, or side of the wall. A variation in grout-joint width of only 1/8 inch over an 8-foot span will not be noticeable.

If the variation is greater than 1/8 inch, either taper-cut the last row of tiles, or, if the last row is a row of full tiles, conceal the uneven grout joint with molding or baseboard that overlaps the last row of tiles and is wide enough to cover the tapered gap.

Adjusting Floor Layout

The procedure for floors is basically the same as that for walls, but you can use actual tiles to experiment with layouts. If your tile is not lugged, plastic tile spacers are extremely helpful. Spacers placed at corners keep tiles aligned and ensure a true, square layout.

Starting at the intersection of the reference lines, place tiles and spacers on floor and note where tiles will have to be cut at ends of rows and around obstacles. The entire area does not have to be covered; just check a couple of rows in each direction and the areas around built-in counters and other obstacles. Be careful not to step on dry tiles while you are doing the layout because they break easily.

If you find that tiles at ends of rows have to be cut to less than one third the width of a full tile, move reference lines one way or the other until you find a better solution.

Problems with square. The best way to lay out a floor that is out of square is to use taper-cut tiles to fill in around all edges.

If you have to correct with tapering cuts, keep in mind that larger pieces of tile will mask an out-of-square situation better than small ones.

A practical modern kitchen is warmed by the charm of colorful pottery and copper molds and utensils. In keeping with the decor, tiles are modeled on traditional Dutch styles. By 1625 tile manufacturing was burgeoning in the towns of Rotterdam, Haarlem, Delft, Gouda, and Amsterdam. Each town established its own style. Tiles from Delft commonly had dark blue, corner rosettes or petal motifs. Accent tiles featured flowers, fruits, and animals.

Adjusting Countertop Layout

Generally, countertops are small enough to do a complete dry-tile layout. Tape corner tiles and bullnose tiles around recessed sinks in place while determining the layout.

Different countertops require slightly different layout approaches.

Straight run. Start at center of front edge. Place field tiles parallel to nosing tiles; work toward back wall.

L-shaped. Begin placing field tiles as shown in the illustration on page 54. This will avoid having cut tiles in the corner.

U-shaped. Begin in the same place as for an L-shaped counter and hope that you reach the next turn with a full tile. If you don't, adjust width of grout joints.

Solid-surface island. On an island counter without sink or cooktop cut-outs, begin field tile placement at the measured centerpoint. Work toward nosing tiles in all directions.

If the existing top is not square or not quite large enough to accommodate the ideal tile layout, it is a simple matter to replace the top.

Island with inserts. Start at outer edges and work toward the cutout for sink or stove. This way cut tile edges will be covered by the fixture.

Backsplash. Extend grout lines so they align with those on the countertop. If you will be using cove tiles, tape them temporarily in place during layout.

Problems with square. There are several ways to adjust for a counter that is out of square; choose the one that fits your particular situation.

Generally it is best to lay out a countertop so that the cut tiles are along the back edge. Other possibilities include making a separate backsplash and fastening it to the countertop at an angle that will correct the square; making adjustments at the front edge by attaching a tapered piece of trim; or removing the existing countertop and resetting or replacing it so that it is square.

If the counter includes a cooktop or a surface-mounted sink, you can start by placing full tiles at the edges of the countertop and working toward the cutout. This way, cut edges of tiles will be hidden beneath the fixture. Realize, however, that grout lines may not be parallel with edges of fixture and that you may have partial tiles in the center of any row that is not interrupted by the cutout.

Finalizing the Layout

When satisfied with your layout, make notes about anything that will help during the installation. These notes can be made on your plan view drawing (see page 22); on the tile (using a piece of tape, color-coded stickers, or a felt-tip pen); or directly on the setting surface (but remember that you will be covering this with adhesive).

Irregularly Shaped Tiles

Laying out irregularly shaped pavers, flagstone, or slate requires plotting additional reference lines.

Measure several tiles to ascertain an average width and length. Decide on an average grout-joint width and then calculate the dimensions of a square section into which 9 or 16 of your tiles will fit.

Starting at the intersection of the main reference lines, divide the area to be tiled into sections of the size determined above. When installing the tiles, make sure they are evenly spaced within each section. (Uneven grout lines are perfectly acceptable when a floor is set with irregularly shaped tiles.)

Diagonal Installations

To install tile on the diagonal, you will need diagonal reference lines.

Start by marking the usual vertical and horizontal lines. Then attach a pencil to one end of a length of string and a pushpin to the other end. The exact length of string is not important (about 4 feet should be adequate for most installations). What is important is that you use the same piece for all of the following measurements.

Insert pushpin at the point where vertical and horizontal reference lines meet. With the pencil, make a mark on each of the four lines radiating from the center; the marks must be equidistant from the center. Remove pushpin and reposition it at one of these marks. Draw a wide arc as shown in the illustration.

Remove pushpin, reposition at another mark and draw an arc that crosses the first one. Repeat until you have four sets of intersecting arcs. When you snap chalk lines through both sets of opposing arcs, you will have diagonal reference lines. If you want to double-check them, the angle between the diagonal lines and the original reference lines should measure 45 degrees.

Special Projects

Apart from walls, floors, and countertops, there are many other uses for tile, including hearths and fireplace surrounds, tabletops, and planters. Although these are common tile installations, specific layout principles are not discussed because each situation is unique. Instead, use the general wall, floor, and countertop layout principles discussed above.

When flowing tile through separate rooms it is important to do a careful layout. Decide how the grid of the tiles will best complement the angles of architectural elements and cabinetry.

Marking Diagonal Reference Lines

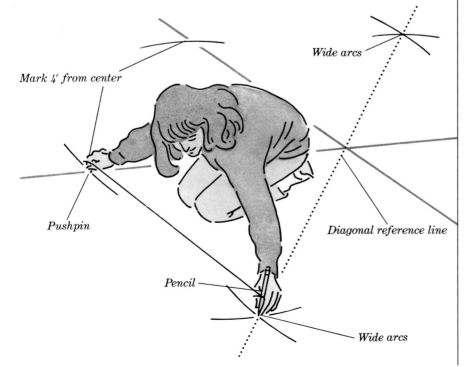

Wide arcs

Mark 4' from center

Pushpin

Pencil

Diagonal reference line

Wide arcs

CUTTING TOOLS

Tile cutting is an easy operation that can be mastered with a bit of practice. Operating most tile-cutting equipment requires a minimum of expertise.

Even the power saws used for cutting tile are not nearly as dangerous as wood-cutting saws. However, standard safety precautions should always be followed.

Use only equipment designed especially for cutting tile, and read the instructions that come with the tool you use. Because tile chips can fly (even when cutting with tile nippers), wear protective glasses or goggles. If using power equipment, wear ear protection as well.

The four standard tools for cutting tile are tile nippers, snap cutter, wet saw, and dry diamond blades. The choice of equipment depends on the type of tile, the type and number of cuts, and the desired smoothness of the cut edge.

Cutting tools are available at most tile retailers and at equipment rental agencies. Following are general guidelines; manufacturer's instructions for specific tools should be followed to the letter to achieve satisfactory cuts and ensure your safety.

Tile Nippers

This hand tool, which looks something like a pair of pliers, is made specifically for cutting ceramic tiles. One jaw is straight and grips the glazed side of the tile; the other is curved and bites into the bisque.

Tile nippers can be used for any tile cut, but the result will be rough compared with other tile-cutting methods. Cutting tile with nippers is also extremely time-consuming. Nippers are best used to nibble away small cuts and to pull out excess tile from notch cuts. They can also be used to break off pieces of tile that have been scored on a snap cutter.

To use. Holding marked tile in one hand and nippers in the other, position straight jaw on the glazed side, just at the mark, and curved jaw on the back side, slightly behind mark. Pull handles together and jaws will bite through tile.

On straight cuts, begin cutting with the jaws partway into the tile, not right at the edge. Take half-bites along the tile until you are about three fourths of the way across, then begin at the other side and work toward the middle. On round notched cuts, take nibbles with tile nippers, working toward the mark.

When tile is scored on a snap cutter, or when preliminary cuts are made with a wet saw, use nippers to pull cut piece away. Place jaws behind the score, push handles together, and pull.

All edges cut with tile nippers will be rough and should be finished with a tile stone.

Snap Cutter

Using a snap cutter is a two-step process. The first step is to score the tile along the cut mark, and the second is to push the handle down, forcing the tile to fracture along the score.

This table-top tool consists of a frame with a fence (guide bar); a carbide, diamond, or ruby scoring wheel; pads that support the tile; and a device that pushes the tile (the bed) to snap it apart. There are many different types of snap cutters, but they all work on the same principle.

Theoretically, you can use a snap cutter to cut any ceramic tile or paver. However, soft tiles do not snap very well, so experiment (using your tile) before taking the cutter home.

Snap cutters work extremely well for straight cuts as small as ½ inch wide and for diagonal cuts (as long as the cutter bed will accept a diagonally placed tile). They can also be used for scoring more intricate cuts.

Once you get into the rhythm of placing, scoring, and snapping tiles,

Tile Nippers

Mark tile and score area to be cut away

Using nippers break out waste in small nibbles

Snap Cutter

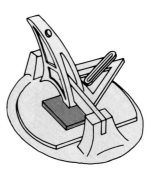

Pull handle across tile to score it. Push down on handle to snap tile

snap cutters work efficiently and effectively. The cut edge is smoother than an edge cut with tile nippers, although not as smooth as one cut by a wet saw.

To use. Place tile on pads, lining up cut mark with guide bar. Many snap cutters have a fence that can be adjusted to hold tile firmly in position. When cutting several tiles to the same size, set this fence and use it as a guide.

Move wheel along cut line with enough pressure to score the glaze. Make only one pass; additional scoring lines may cause tile to shatter. Then lift or press handle (depending on the type of tool). One quick pop should cause the tile to fracture along the score. Smooth with a tile stone.

Wet Saw

A wet saw is a power tool that will cut all kinds of masonry products except pavers embedded with loose stone, which might get caught in the blade. A wet saw produces the finest and smoothest cut of the tools described.

A wet saw is the only tool that will cut rounded trim tiles and soft tiles that cannot be snap cut. It is also used for straight cuts and for short parallel stop cuts that can be smoothed into curves or notches.

The standard components of a wet saw are the trough, a sliding table with an adjustable fence for tile alignment; a diamond-impregnated blade with a small metal rim; two water jets that cool the blade and blow chips out of the way; an insulated motor; and an insulated switch. Wet saws should be plugged into a grounded, three-prong outlet.

Because of the nature of the blade, wet saws are not as dangerous as saws designed for cutting wood. The small diamond chips will cut hard surfaces but not soft ones (like human skin). However, these blades should still be treated with respect.

To use. Place marked tile in position on sliding table and set fences to hold tile in place. If you are cutting several tiles to the same size, keep these fences in position to act as guides. Turn the saw on and slide tile

toward blade. Keep tile flush against table. If it lifts off the guide, it may vibrate when it comes in contact with the blade, which will cause it to shatter and fly apart. Be careful to keep your fingers away from the blade as you push tile through saw.

When cutting shaped tiles set a block of wood in the curve. This will keep vibration to a minimum.

Dry Diamond Blades

Diamond-impregnated or carbon-tipped blades can turn regular tools into tile cutters. These blades can be mounted on hand-held grinders and used to cut tiles as well as to cut away tile and grout that you want to remove. The cuts may be rather jagged, but if they will not show, or if a jagged edge is not a problem (on pavers, for example), a grinder can be used effectively.

Dry diamond blades can also be mounted on power saws or on a hacksaw handle. A hacksaw makes it easy to cut circles or other shapes out of the middle of a tile (see illustration on page 63). Although hand-sawing is time-consuming, you'll have more control over the cut than you would with a power saw. However, the finished edge will not be as smooth.

To use. Place marked tile in a vise to hold it steady while you cut. The blade will cut quickly through the tile but many tile chips will fly; be sure to wear safety goggles.

Tile Stone

Use a Carborundum℗ stone or a small piece of concrete to smooth cut edges and curves and to create angled edges on uncut tiles. Although the quality of edge produced will not be the same as that of a factory-finished tile, duplicating the contour of a bullnose tile, for example, will make the job look more professional.

To use. Sand edges with short strokes. Avoid rubbing across or scratching tile surface as you work.

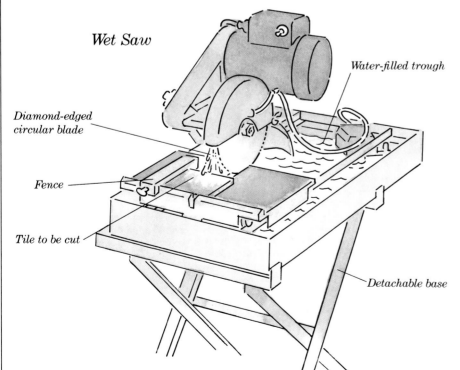

Wet Saw

Water-filled trough

Diamond-edged circular blade

Fence

Tile to be cut

Detachable base

MARKING & CUTTING TILE

Even the simplest tile project requires cutting some tiles to fit. If you did a complete and accurate dry-tile layout, you can make all necessary cuts prior to setting any tiles.

However, in most cases it is advisable to mark and cut tiles only after the full tiles are installed. This way you are sure to get an exact fit.

Marking Tiles for Cutting

In order for a cut tile to fit correctly, it must be marked correctly. There are no absolute rules; you merely make enough notations on the tile itself to ensure an accurate cut. Following are a few pointers.

On glazed tiles, use a fine-tip felt pen to mark cut lines. On unglazed tiles, which might absorb ink, use a scratching tool such as a nail, or attach a piece of tape to the tile and mark the tape with pen, pencil, or grease pencil. The latter method is suitable for any masonry product.

When an entire row of cut tiles is required, do not assume that each tile should be cut to the same size. Check the distance between the last set tile and the wall (or edge) at several points along the row.

Indicate anything you feel will be helpful while cutting. For example, draw a scribble across what will be the waste area so that you know on which side to allow for the amount lost by the saw cut.

Code marked tiles as to their locations. Remember to write the code in an area that will not be cut off.

When marking tiles with ridged backs, be sure that cut lines are parallel to ridges.

Drawing Cut Lines

The following are specific descriptions of how to mark tiles in order to fit them accurately around different obstacles you may encounter.

Wall and floor edges. Simply measure the distance between wall edge and last tile set (remembering to take the width of grout joints into account). Or use the following method: Set tile to be cut exactly on top of last full tile that was set. Place a shim equivalent to width of two grout lines vertically against the wall, and then set a marker tile on top of the other two tiles and butt it against shim. Using top tile as a straightedge, draw cut line on middle tile.

Corners. Use the straight-cut method twice, once for each side.

Around fixtures. These can be marked by measuring the distance from last set tile to edge of fixture and marking that measurement on the tile to be cut. Since cut edges will be covered by escutcheons, these small cuts need not be exact.

Diagonal lines. Use a sliding bevel square (a small hand-held tool that duplicates angles). Adjust square to necessary angle and transfer this angle to tile.

Complicated shapes. If you need to mark a tile to fit around objects with complicated shapes, such as intricate wood molding, either make a cardboard pattern or use a contour gauge. This tool consists of a handle and a series of attached rods. When pushed against a surface, the rods duplicate the shape of that surface. Once rods are set, lock handle in place, then use gauge to mark tile.

Fitting Border Tiles

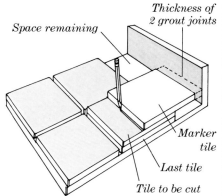

Space remaining

Thickness of 2 grout joints

Marker tile

Last tile

Tile to be cut

Cutting Tiles

Some tile stores will cut tiles for customers. If you use this service, you will need to be especially accurate and clear when marking tiles for cutting. Be sure to indicate which is the waste portion of the tile. Remember also to code the tiles as to their locations so you know where each one belongs when you bring them back.

Consider using a cutting service if you need only a few cuts or if the cuts are intricate. In most cases, repeated trips to have tiles cut will be more time-consuming than learning how to cut them yourself.

Many tile suppliers lend or rent cutting tools; these tools can also be obtained from equipment rental agencies.

Common Tile Cuts

Successful cutting is not difficult as long as you have the proper tools, some practice, and an accurately measured and marked tile. See Cutting Tools, page 60, for descriptions of the tools mentioned below and instructions for their use.

Straight cut. Make one cut with a wet saw, snap cutter, or tile nippers.

Short cut. Make one cut with a snap cutter; or cut with tile nippers; or score with snap cutter and break off with tile nippers.

Notched cut. Make several cuts with a wet saw, then use tile nippers to pry out notch.

Round notched cut. Nibble away area with tile nippers, then smooth with a tile stone to round out shape. You can also make several cuts of different lengths with a wet saw and smooth them with a tile stone, but tile nippers will work better.

Nibble cut. Take several small bites with tile nippers. Continue until notch is desired size. Smooth with a tile stone.

Diagonal cut or miter cut. Make one cut with a wet saw or with a snap cutter that has a bed equipped to hold a tile on the diagonal.

Stepped cut. Make a series of straight cuts with a wet saw.

Corner cut. Make two cuts with a wet saw or a snap cutter.

Round cut. Set tile in vise. Drill starter hole with carbon-tip bit on electric drill. Using a hacksaw fitted with a tile-cutting blade, saw rounded shape. (Slip hacksaw blade through drilled hole before attaching blade to handle.) An alternative method is to cut the tile in half and make round notched cuts in each half.

Cutting Stone and Pavers

Marble, granite, slate, quarry tiles, and other pavers should be marked in the same manner as ceramic tiles. A wet saw is the best tool for accomplishing accurate and smooth cuts on all finished stone and pavers.

If a stone tile is thin, it may cut easily with a snap cutter. However, stone is a natural product that has a grain. If the score runs across the grain, the fracture is likely to follow the grain rather than the score. Experience is the best indicator of whether a snap cutter will work with the product you are using.

If a paver is very dense and thin enough to fit into the frame, it should cut with a snap cutter.

If your installation does not require straight-line cuts (randomly set patio stone, for example), a rough cut may be all that is required. For a finished edge, cut the stone with a wet saw.

A dry diamond blade will cut finished stone and pavers. If you have only a few cuts to make, consider attaching this type of blade to a hacksaw. Set the tile in a vise to hold it steady while you cut.

For small cuts on dimensioned stone and pavers, use tile nippers and smooth the edge with a tile stone.

Cutting Sheet-mounted Tiles

Some mosaic tiles and tile panels are sold mounted on a mesh backing. These should be separated from each other with shears or a utility knife before you cut them. Cut as you would any other tile, then trim away excess backing material. If using a wet saw, pull backing off separated tiles before making the cut.

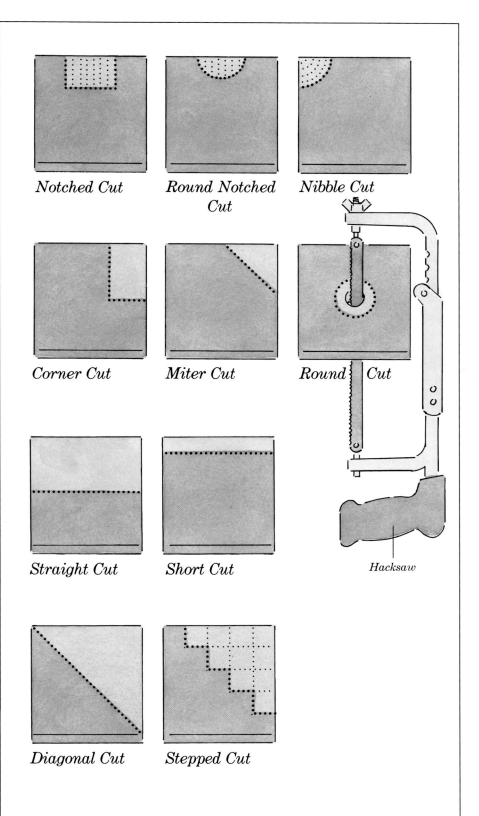

Notched Cut

Round Notched Cut

Nibble Cut

Corner Cut

Miter Cut

Round Cut

Straight Cut

Short Cut

Hacksaw

Diagonal Cut

Stepped Cut

THINSETTING TOOLS

Adhesive must be precisly applied to form the best bond and provide a quality tile installation.

What You Will Need

There are some special tools needed to apply thinset correctly and others that will help with setting tiles. None of these tools are difficult to use.

Alignment Tools

You'll need the same straightedge and carpenter's level used during layout to check tile alignment that tiles are flush. You can use your jury stick (see page 52) as a substitute for either or both of these tools.

Beater Board

Once tiles are aligned, you'll need a beater board or a rubber mallet to push the tiles firmly into the adhesive. A beater board is simply a 6- to 8-inch block of plywood, one side of which is covered with felt or old carpet. Use a hammer with the beater board.

A rubber mallet serves the same purpose as a beater board, and may be easier to use because it allows you to see better than does a beater board. If you have a mallet or want to invest in one, use it. If not, a beater board is a good homemade equivalent.

Dress Code

Wear a charcoal-filter dust mask and rubber gloves when mixing and applying thinset. Wear loose, comfortable clothes. Avoid long sleeves, which might slip into the adhesive. If you are setting a tile floor, consider using knee pads to save your joints while you work.

Cover-ups

Be sure to have plenty of plastic sheets or drop cloths to cover surrounding surfaces and have some

masking tape handy to mask plumbing fixtures. Masking tape is also used to hold vertical and edging tiles in place while the adhesive cures. Keep plenty of sponges or rags nearby for cleaning up.

Mixing Bucket

You'll need a good-sized, sturdy bucket to mix thinset in. Later, it can be cleaned and used for mixing grout. Consider your water source when choosing a bucket. Be sure it will fit under the closest faucet because you will probably need to mix several bucketfuls of setting materials.

Mixing Paddles

Only a stirring stick is needed to stir organic mastic. Mix small amounts of thinset adhesives (1 to 2 gallons) with a plastic or wooden stirring paddle. For larger amounts use electric mortar mixing paddles, which can be rented at most equipment rental agencies. You can attach paddles to a standard home drill or rent the entire

Beater Board

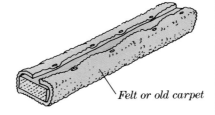

Felt or old carpet

Tile Spacers

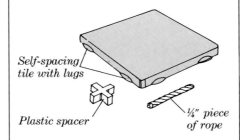

Self-spacing tile with lugs

Plastic spacer

¼" piece of rope

piece of equipment. Mortar mixing paddles are designed specifically for mixing mortar for tile setting. Other mixing paddles, such as those for mixing paint, operate at too fast a speed to mix thinset properly.

Notched Trowels

Perhaps the most important tool used in thinsetting is the notched trowel. A notched trowel looks like most other trowels except that there are notches along one long side and usually both short sides. The smooth side is used to spread the adhesive, the notched sides for combing the adhesive so that the tile will bond effectively to the thinset.

Notched trowels are available with a variety of notch sizes for applying different types of adhesives and installing different types of tiles. The adhesive product label and tile store personnel should be able to assist you in the trowel selection. Most ceramic tile adhesives are applied with a ¼-inch notched trowel.

Notched trowels can be cleaned and used again. If you do not expect to do a lot of tile installation and do not want to invest in a lot of thinsetting equipment, less expensive disposable, plastic notched trowels are available. Although they are not quite as sturdy as the metal varieties, they function acceptably for most thinsetting applications.

Tile Spacers

Tile spacers are small plastic pieces used to determine grout joint widths during tile alignment. (You can also use tile spacers to assist you during layout.) Tile spacers come in a variety of sizes and shapes to match various joint widths and types of tile. They are available anywhere tile is sold. Pieces of cut wood can be substituted for the plastic spacers. If you are setting lugged tiles, you will not need tile spacers.

Utility Knife

Use a utility or razor knife to clean hardened thinset out of joints before applying grout.

INSTALLATION TECHNIQUES

*T*he instructions that follow refer to what is called a thinset or thin-bed installation. This means that tiles are attached to the substrate with a thinset adhesive.

These adhesive products have virtually eliminated the need to set tile in a mortar bed and have made tile setting an easy-to-master project.

Use these general guidelines regardless of whether the tile job is a wall, floor, countertop, or special project, or whether the installation will be indoors or outdoors, or whether you are using ceramic tiles or stone products, tile panels, mosaics, quarry pavers, or irregular stone pavers. Special precautions and exceptions regarding materials other than glazed ceramic tile are described on page 69.

Before you start setting tiles, make sure surfaces are prepared, layout is satisfactorily completed, and all tools and materials are on hand.

Site Conditions

The ideal job-site temperature is 65° to 75° F. In cold weather the adhesive may take as long as a week to cure; if it is very cold, the liquid in the adhesive will freeze and no bonding will take place. If the temperature is too high, moisture in the adhesive will be absorbed too quickly, the cure will be irregular, and the bond will be weak.

For indoor installations, adjust the thermostat to maintain a constant temperature during setting and curing periods. Avoid using an air conditioner as the dehumidifier will absorb moisture in the adhesive too quickly.

When working outdoors, set tile in the early evening so that the sun does not dry the adhesive too quickly.

Precautions

To ensure that your tile-setting project goes smoothly and safely, take the following precautions before beginning to work.
☐ Remove nearby plumbing fixtures or use tape to mask them.
☐ Cover all surrounding surfaces with drop cloths.
☐ Have all tiling materials and tools on hand.
☐ Be sure that the job site is well ventilated.
☐ Wear rubber gloves and a charcoal-filter dust mask while working with all thinset adhesives, and do not smoke near these chemicals.
☐ Wear comfortable clothing while setting tile.

Tile-setting Procedure

All tile setting is merely a repetition of these simple steps:
1. Mix enough adhesive for a small section.
2. Apply adhesive to section.
3. Position and align tiles.
4. Bed and level tiles.

Perform these four steps for each section. Then, when the entire area is complete and the adhesive has cured, finish the installation by grouting and sealing.

Although the steps are simple, read through this section completely before beginning your project.

Mixing Adhesive

The amount of adhesive needed for a tile installation is determined by the square footage of the surface to be covered. Product labels usually list estimated coverage. Purchase plenty of adhesive in advance so you don't have to interrupt your tile-setting job with a trip to the store.

Organic mastics (see page 42) are purchased premixed and should be stirred before application. Other thinset adhesives consist of a combination of liquid and dry materials that must be mixed at the job site.

Ratios of liquid to dry ingredients vary depending on the product but will be listed on the label. Do not mix more adhesive than you will be able to spread and cover with tile in about one hour. If adhesive begins to harden in the mixing bucket while you are working, it may have begun to cure. Do not attempt to thin it with water or other liquid as this may affect the bond; discard it and mix a new batch.

Measure liquid ingredients into a mixing bucket first, then slowly add measured amount of dry ingredients. Stir by hand with a plastic or wood paddle or with special electric mortar-mixing paddles, which can be rented at most equipment rental agencies. Whether mixing by hand or machine, be sure to keep paddles submerged. Lifting them out introduces air into the adhesive, lessening its bonding ability. Adhesive is thoroughly mixed when all dry ingredients are incorporated and it falls off, but does not run off, the mixing stick.

Let mixed adhesive rest for about 10 minutes before applying.

Applying Adhesive

Adhesive is applied in two steps: First it is spread, then combed. Use a notched trowel for both steps.

Most adhesive applications require using a ¼-inch notched trowel, but the exact size depends on the weight of your tile and the type of adhesive used. Recommendations are listed on product labels.

Apply adhesive to an area small enough to be covered with tiles during the "open time" of the adhesive. Open time, usually listed on the adhesive label, is the amount of time you have to set tiles into spread adhesive. Begin by working in a one- to three-foot-square section. As you become more proficient, the size of the working area can be increased.

Stir rested adhesive once or twice. Scoop a small amount onto flat surface of trowel. Hold trowel with the smooth surface at an angle of about 30 degrees relative to the surface to be tiled. Press adhesive firmly onto surface, using a sweeping motion and making sure all areas are equally covered and no air bubbles have formed. Be careful not to cover reference lines. Turn trowel so that notched edge is held at an angle of about 45 degrees and comb the spread adhesive. Comb in two passes to make a crosshatch pattern.

Testing the Coverage

The quality of the tile bond depends on using the correct amount of adhesive; this amount varies depending on the weight of the tile and on whether the tile has a smooth back or is grooved.

To test the coverage, place a tile in the spread and combed adhesive. Push down gently with a slight twisting motion. Remove your hand for a moment, then carefully lift tile up again. Check back of tile: It should be well covered with adhesive. If any bisque shows through, the ridges in the adhesive are too shallow and you need to apply more adhesive and hold trowel at a wider angle while combing. If adhesive has piled up or pushed well over the sides of the tile, ridges are too deep and trowel should be held at a narrower angle while combing.

Positioning Field Tiles

Once you are confident that the adhesive is spread and combed correctly, begin setting tiles in place. Begin at intersection of reference lines. Place tiles onto adhesive firmly and with a slight twisting motion. If using spacers, butt them against corners of tiles as you work. If not, tiles should be placed accurately but not necessarily exactly; it is more important to cover the adhesive quickly than to finalize tile placement.

Aligning Tiles

After covering spread adhesive with tiles, begin adjusting them. Use the reference lines as guides for row alignment and the jury stick, tile spacers, or both for individual tile placement.

Bedding and Leveling

After a section is accurately positioned, make sure that tiles are flush, level, and firmly set in the adhesive. Place beater board against them and, using a hammer, tap it lightly several times. Remove board and use the jury stick, a carpenter's level, or both to check that tiles are flush and set into adhesive evenly. You may have to work around or reposition spacers in order to lay the beater across the surface of a row of tiles.

If the spacers stick up above the surface of the tiles and prevent the use of a beater board, you can use a rubber mallet either alone or in conjunction with a leveling board to level tiles. (If it is long enough, the jury stick can double as a leveling device.) Set leveling board across the surface of about six to eight tiles. Tap board with mallet along the entire length, then check to see that surface of each tile is making contact with the board. Also check the surface with a carpenter's level. Make any necessary adjustments so that tiles are flush and level in all directions.

Completing the Field

Continue spreading and combing adhesive onto small sections and setting, aligning, bedding, and leveling tiles until all field tiles are in place. Be careful not to disturb a set area as you continue tile installation. Check alignment and level across each section and between sections as you proceed. Wipe excess adhesive from tile surfaces and clean up any spills as soon as possible. Although cleaning solvents are listed on product labels, all thinset adhesives are difficult to remove once they have hardened.

Installing Cut Tile

Once you have finished setting all full tiles, you will probably need to cut some tiles to fit around edges, fixtures, or other obstacles. When you are satisfied that tiles are cut correctly, set them in place.

Because it is generally impossible to trowel on adhesive for this final row, edging tiles and V-caps (as well as handmade tiles with uneven backs, ceramic accessories, small and difficult-to-reach field tiles, and some mosaic tile sheets) require a two-step adhesive application known as back-buttering.

Back-buttering

Using the smooth edge of the trowel, first apply a thin coat of adhesive to the back of the tile. Next add an extra layer of adhesive to cushion the installation, and set tile firmly in place. When you have positioned several tiles, align them and bed them into the adhesive with a beater board or mallet until they are flush with surrounding tiles. Check alignment with a leveling board and a carpenter's level.

Set all cut tiles, trim tiles, and ceramic accessories to complete the tile installation.

Use masking tape to hold tiles in place on vertical surfaces or edges. Allow adhesive to cure.

Curing

Curing time is the length of time it takes for all moisture to evaporate from the adhesive, allowing it to harden and bond tile to backing. Curing time varies according to the product used, but it is generally about 24 hours.

Keep the area ventilated while adhesive cures. If more than one surface in a room is to be tiled, complete all tile setting and all curing before grouting and sealing.

Installing Wall Tiles

Starting at the center, begin setting full tiles along the horizontal reference line. Unless you are absolutely sure of your layout, it is best to set all full tiles first and then go back and measure, cut, and set all cut tiles.

Tiling More than One Wall

Corners should have been laid out so that the horizontal grout joints on both walls will align. On inside corners, set cut tiles against each other, allowing room for a grout joint. On outside corners, lap bullnose tiles over unfinished edges of tiles on adjoining wall, or use a row of trim tile and butt tiles on both walls to it.

Installing Accessories

The most common ceramic wall accessories are soap dishes, toothbrush holders, and towel bars, all of which are sold to match common-size wall tiles. These can be installed in one of three ways, depending on the accessory: Recessed into the wall, as part of the tile installation, or on top of the installed tile.

Safety bars. Note that safety bars, and any accessory that is intended to be used as a grab bar, should be nonceramic and must be firmly anchored into wall framing.

Recessed Accessories

To install recessed and semi-recessed accessories, cut a hole in backing surface large enough to accommodate accessory. Most of these accessories come with a wire basket or means of support for the adhesive. Install this support, then apply adhesive to both the accessory and the substrate. Set the accessory in place, being careful to apply pressure evenly when fitting tile into support so you don't crack surrounding tiles.

Surface-mounted Accessories

When installing surface-mounted ceramic accessories using a thinset installation method, check the accessory manufacturer's label for adhesive recommendations. In wet areas, install accessories with special moisture-proof adhesives.

Install surface accessories after all field tiles are set and adhesive has cured, but prior to grouting. Make sure the exact position of the accessory tile is marked on the substrate and masked before you install field tiles. This way you can tile without getting adhesive on accessory areas.

Remove any masking from backing surface, and make sure surface is clean and dry. Most accessories are designed with protrusions along the back that are pushed into the wall and act as anchors. Drill holes for these protrusions through any backing material and into substrate.

Spread adhesive on the back of the accessory—including the protrusions—as well as on the substrate. Insert accessory in desired location and press firmly for about 10 seconds. Clean excess adhesive from edges of grout joints. Support accessory with masking tape until adhesive cures completely.

Tile-top Accessories

These accessories are usually attached to the wall with screws. Drill screw holes through tile and backing material and into wallboard to ensure that accessories are set into a solid backing. When drilling tile, use a carbide bit, work slowly, and keep drizzling water in the hole as you drill.

Installing Wall Tiles

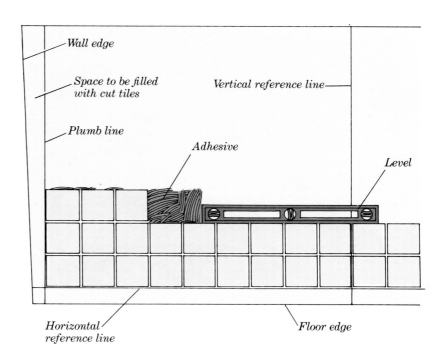

Wall edge

Space to be filled with cut tiles

Vertical reference line

Plumb line

Adhesive

Level

Horizontal reference line

Floor edge

Establishing Full Tile Area

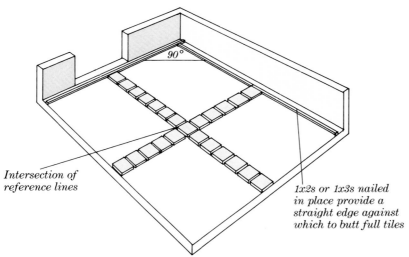

90°

*Intersection of
reference lines*

*1x2s or 1x3s nailed
in place provide a
straight edge against
which to butt full tiles*

Working Out From Corner

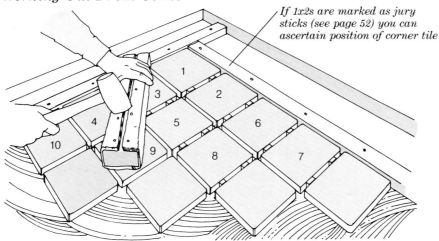

*If 1x2s are marked as jury
sticks (see page 52) you can
ascertain position of corner tile*

Tiled Baseboard

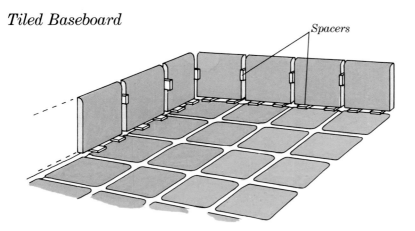

Spacers

Tiling Floors

You've heard about never painting yourself into a corner? Well, you don't want to tile yourself into a corner, either. Before beginning a floor tile installation, evaluate your exits. Most damage to floor tiles occurs between initial setting and grouting. Walking on freshly installed floors can break tiles and dislodge them from the adhesive, breaking the bond. Plan your installation so that you avoid standing on just-set tiles and crossing the floor before the installation is complete. Use plywood "stepping stones" if you must use the floor prior to grouting. Walk carefully and recheck tile alignment if you feel any movement as you walk.

Begin laying tiles where reference lines intersect. Install tiles according to the directions on page 65. Install all full field tiles, matching corners so they are aligned properly. When all full tiles are set, measure, cut, and set the cut tiles.

After adhesive has cured completely, grout as directed on page 77. However, do not grout joints next to walls and cabinets. Instead, fill these with caulk, which has expansion properties that grout does not have. If there is any movement between cabinets and floor or between walls and floor, the caulk will prevent the joint from cracking and allowing moisture to penetrate into the tile work.

Installing Tile Baseboard Trim

Instead of a wood or vinyl baseboard, you may wish to use tile that matches or coordinates with floor tiles. If you do so, use bullnose tiles so that the visible upper edge of the baseboard is a finished one. Spread adhesive on the back of the tiles and set in place. Align grout joints between baseboard tiles so that they match those on floor.

Installing Pavers

Install pavers using any thinset adhesive. Because they are usually slightly irregular by design, you may need to spread a layer of adhesive on the back before setting the paver into the adhesive spread on the substrate.

Coat pavers with a penetrating sealer prior to grouting. Apply more—either a penetrating or a coating sealer—after the grout has cured.

Installing Dimensioned Stone

Dimensioned stone is installed using the same techniques as for ceramic tile. There are, however, a few special warnings that apply only to dimensioned stone.

The substrate must be absolutely sound and solid, with very little flex. The adhesive used must be suitable for natural stone. It should not be petroleum based (which may stain) or water based (which will not form a strong enough bond), but rather a special marble mastic or a urethane epoxy. The warping and blistering often seen on stone installations (especially on green marble) is caused by using water-based adhesive.

Stone tiles can be cut using a wet saw for most cuts and tile nippers for small cuts.

The width of the grout joints varies with the look required. Use sanded grouts when the joint is ⅛ inch thick or wider and nonsanded grouts for smaller joints. For best results, use a latex additive with a portland-cement grout. Finished grout joints should be smooth, hard, dense, and filled to the top of the tile. Do not use silicone caulk around dimensioned stone.

Honed and flamed dimensioned stone will often benefit aesthetically from sealing. Check product labels for appropriate products to use with natural stone. Use penetrating sealers over the entire installation about 28 days after installation is completed.

Circular forms work well to enclose a distinct space, such as the seating area of a tile-covered deck. This installation is also practical because the additional grout needed to fill curved joints provides a non-skid surface.

Establishing Layout

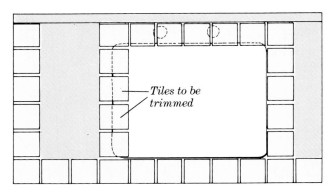

Tiles to be trimmed

Installing Tile

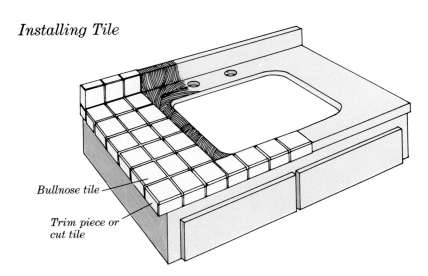

Bullnose tile

Trim piece or cut tile

Grouting

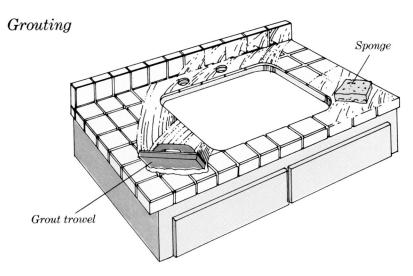

Sponge

Grout trowel

Tiling Countertops

Countertops should be tiled with glazed or semi-vitreous tile, especially around sinks, food-preparation areas, and any area that will get wet. Unglazed and vitreous tiles are not appropriate for this use as they will absorb moisture and will stain.

For all countertop installations in wet areas, plan to use latex additives in both adhesive and grout.

Purchase tiles rated for use on horizontal surfaces; they are thicker than those made for wall installations. (Ceramic tiles for use on walls are usually ¼ inch thick; for horizontal surfaces, ½ inch thick.) Ceramic countertop tiles are sold individually and in panels. Polished dimensioned stone that is ⅜ inch thick can also be used for countertops.

Cooktops, sinks, faucets, and kitchen accessories must be taken into account when designing a tiled countertop. Changing or adding these elements after the tile is in place can result in extra work and damaged tile. If your countertop contains a recessed sink, install the sink prior to setting tile. If the sink is surface mounted, install it on top of the tile after grouting.

Countertop tile installations require the same basic steps as any other tile-setting job; these are described on page 65. Work from front to back on countertops backed by a wall, and from the center outward on island counters. Set all full tiles first and then measure, cut, and install the cut tiles.

Setting Backsplash Tiles

Install tiles on the backsplash or wall behind the countertop after counter tiles are set but before grouting. Tiles for backsplashes are installed in the same manner as wall tiles (see page 67). Make sure that the vertical grout joints on the backsplash will align with grout lines on countertop.

If your backsplash will stop short of the overhead cabinets, the installation will look neater with a final row of full tiles. Either use bullnose tiles or plan to add some kind of trim. If the backsplash will extend all the way to the cabinets, a final row of cut tiles will not be noticeable.

Begin tiling at the countertop edge, using cove tiles if you prefer a rounded corner to a right-angled one. (A rounded corner is easier to clean.) Avoid getting adhesive on the wall above the area to be tiled.

When you have finished tiling, you may need to use masking tape to hold backsplash tiles in place while adhesive cures. When adhesive has set, mask joint between backsplash and counter. Grout backsplash and countertop at the same time. Then remove tape and fill joint between the two with caulk.

Attaching Nonceramic Trim

There are many nonceramic trims available for edging a tiled countertop; the most common ones are made of plastic or wood. In some cases using these will make it unnecessary to attach a nosing strip to the plywood base prior to tiling.

Plastic edging strips are available in a wide variety of colors and sizes, and are used most effectively as substitutes for bullnose trim. The strips are glued in place with regular thinset adhesive.

Wood trim is a popular and good-looking edging for a ceramic-tile countertop. However, because wood expands when wet, special care must be taken during installation. Paint all sides of wood trim with one or two coats of water sealant before attaching to countertop. Bed the wood trim in caulk and attach it to the plywood substrate with screws spaced about six inches apart and bored deep enough to hold trim securely to plywood. Plug screw holes. Wood trim requires occasional resealing.

Installing a Chopping Block

A wood chopping block set into a tiled countertop is both attractive and useful. However, it must be properly installed or water may seep underneath and damage the substrate.

Buy a chopping block slightly larger than the desired size. Cut it to a size that will fit into your tile pattern, allowing a ⅛-inch expansion gap on all sides. After installing tile but before grouting, attach block to substrate with glue and screws driven in from underneath. Position chopping block so that the top surface is about ⅛ inch higher than the tile surface. This will avoid scratching the tile.

Let adhesive dry, grout tile, then caulk around the chopping block.

A white stripe streaks across the vanity. It ties in with the white cabinetry and basin and crisply contrasts the gray-tiled countertop.

INSTALLING ACCENT TILES

Decorative or accent tiles—around a door or window frame, along a roof line, on stair risers, or behind a wood-burning stove—add architectural interest.

Read the general sections on substrates, layout, and installation techniques, in addition to the specific information below, before beginning your tile installation.

Walls

Accent tiles on walls can be installed in two ways: On top of an existing wall in the same manner as any wall installation, or flush with the wall.

You can install accent tiles on top of any sound, smooth, clean, flat surface. Organic mastic is a good choice of adhesive for this small amount of tile work. If you are installing individual accent tiles, use the back-butter method and be careful to clean up any adhesive that oozes from behind the tile onto the wall. You won't need to grout around individual tiles.

To install accent tiles on an uneven surface—an exterior stucco wall, for instance—first glue or screw a piece of exterior-grade plywood, cut to size, to the wall. Then attach tiles to plywood using standard thinsetting techniques for applying tile to a wall.

To install accent tiles flush with an existing wall, rout out the finish wall material behind the intended location of the tiles, attach tiles with thinset adhesive following the general guidelines for applying tile to a wall, and use grout to fill in space between tile and edge of wall. On a new wall, plan the tile installation before finishing the backing so tile will end up flush with finished wall.

Shielding the area on and around fireplaces was one of the many uses for tiles fired in the pottery shops of the town of Delft during the seventeenth century. Modern interpretations of delft motifs surround this indoor grill.

Signage

Name and address tiles are an increasingly popular choice for both personal and commercial signs. It is recommended that these tiles be installed on a plywood backing. A piece of plywood bolted to a wall is much easier to remove when you move or remodel than are tiles installed directly on the wall.

Cut a piece of exterior-grade plywood to size and attach it to the wall. Then use standard thinset adhesive techniques to install tiles. Use an edging tile or wood trim to finish the edge of the plywood.

Door Frames & Windowsills

Tile can be used very effectively to surround a door or window either indoors or outdoors. It will take the place of and be far more decorative than conventional wood trim pieces. Use bullnose or special tiles called windowsills to decorate sills. Set tiles so that rounded edges face outward. If the wall is also tiled, either set windowsill tiles last so that the finished edge of the sill tile is set on top of the wall tile or start at the window to make sure you do not have to cut frame pieces. Use the same setting materials and techniques as for any wall installation.

Above: Tile wainscoting is just as effective outdoors as it is indoors. Extending the trim tile up and around the door frame maintains the continuity of the design.
Right: Lining window ledges with colorful ceramics provides a view that can be enjoyed from inside and out.
Top right: Emphasize and enliven a simple doorway by framing it with a tiled border. The same treatment can be applied to a window frame.

Fireplaces & Stoves

Before installing tiles around fireplaces, wood-burning stoves, and other heat-generating elements, check local building codes concerning requirements for incorporating fire-resistant materials between the tile work and any combustible wall (including standard wallboard). You may have to incorporate an air channel behind the tile work. This involves attaching special noncombustible spacers to the wall, attaching a backing material such as CBU (Cementitious Backer Units) to the spacers, and then installing the tile.

The heat generated by fireplaces and stoves can destroy the bond of many adhesives. Organic mastics should never be used for these installations, and some thinset adhesives should be avoided. Check that the chosen adhesive is heat resistant, and for best results use one that is resistant to 400° F.

If the fireplace has a metal face (as zero-clearance fireplaces do) that is too flimsy to support tiles, laminate CBU to the metal first.

As with any wall installation, the backing surface must be clean, smooth, and flat to ensure a successful tile job. If you are tiling around an existing fireplace, be sure to completely clean all soot from the surface prior to applying thinset. Any traces of soot will prevent a proper bond.

Install a fireplace surround or a wood-burning-stove surround using the same techniques that you would for any wall.

A fireplace surround is an excellent site for using a faux thick-bed wall installation. Faux thick-bed is achieved by attaching extra CBU backing to the wall only in the area that will be covered by tile. This method allows you to use edging tile around the perimeter of your installation.

When tiling a hearth, be sure that your tile can withstand the weight of stacked wood and the occasional pounding of dropped logs and tools.

Above: A ceramic tile installation can become a piece of permanent art. Consider commissioning a local tile artist to produce pieces for your fireplace hearth and chimney breast.
Right: Black marble adds drama to a simple raised fireplace especially when it is showcased between the transparent surfaces of glazed walls.

To strengthen the backing, consider using two pieces of CBU laminated together with thinset adhesive. Install hearth tiles in the same manner as floor tiles, but use a heat-resistant adhesive. If the hearth abuts a wood floor, leave a ⅛-inch gap between tiles and floor and fill it with caulk at the end of your installation job.

Stairs & Risers

For stair treads, use bullnose, step-nosing, or down-angled tiles rated for floor use. Set tiles so that rounded edges are at front of steps. Install tiles in the same manner as for any floor installation.

Stair risers can be set with any field tile and provide an excellent opportunity to use special decorative tiles. Cover the entire riser with tiles, or use the tiles as accent pieces. The step-nosing will hide the top edges of riser tiles.

Install riser tiles in the same manner as wall tiles. If you are tiling the entire stair, install risers first so that finished edge of tread tile will end up on top.

Tabletops

A single tile or field of tiles set into a tabletop is decorative and serves the practical purpose of a built-in trivet. If you are setting individual tiles into a table, you'll have to rout a section of the table surface so that tiles will be flush with tabletop. Attach tiles in the same manner as you would a floor installation.

If you are covering the entire table with tiles, follow instructions for installing an island countertop.

Be creative with your own leftovers or with discount tiles from "the bone piles" found in many tile stores. Set into risers of an outdoor staircase, individual tiles create a patchwork of color.

GROUTING TOOLS

*G*routing is a messy but simple job that can be accomplished with inexpensive and easy-to-obtain tools. If you prefer, you can substitute items you already have around the house—a toothbrush, for example.

Use the same clothing (charcoal-filter dust mask and rubber gloves) worn for thinsetting. In addition you will need the following items.

Grout Trowel

A grout trowel is an inexpensive rubber-faced trowel that is designed specifically for spreading grout. Different grades of rubber are used for grouting different tile surfaces. Never use a steel trowel to spread grout—it may scratch the surface of the tile.

Use the face of the trowel to press grout into joints, and the edge to remove excess grout from the tiles. Grout trowels can be cleaned and used again.

Substitute. The type of squeegee designed for cleaning windows can be used as a substitute for, or in conjunction with, a grout trowel. However, squeegees usually have a much narrower face, so spreading will go much faster with a grout trowel.

Margin Trowel

A margin trowel consists of a 1½- to 2-inch-wide metal blade attached to the handle at a right angle. This tool is used to finish tile joints, especially around edges. The advantage of a margin trowel is that the metal edges will cut a clean line when finishing the joints. Margin trowels are easily cleaned and can be reused.

Substitutes. Instead of a margin trowel, you can use any small metal tool, such as an old butter knife, to finish grout joints. Some people swear by a toothbrush handle.

Whatever finishing tool you choose, use the same one throughout so that the shape of the joints is consistent.

Bucket

Clean the bucket and paddles used to mix adhesive and use them for grouting. Make sure the bucket will fit under the closest faucet because you will be needing many bucketfuls of clean water.

Sponges

Choose a good-quality sponge with rounded corners to clean off excess grout and to finish grout joints. (Square corners can catch in joint lines and pull up the grout.)

Use another clean sponge or a length of cheesecloth to remove the final film from the tile surface.

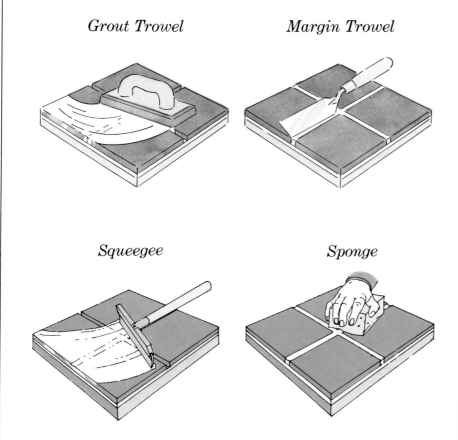

Grout Trowel   *Margin Trowel*

Squeegee   *Sponge*

GROUTING & CAULKING

*A*ccomplishing a high-quality grout job is not difficult; it merely takes patience and some elbow grease. Grouting can even be fun, in a messy kind of way, especially if you enjoyed finger painting as a child.

Grouting

Grout is a type of mortar used to fill the joints between tiles. It protects the edges of the tiles and prevents moisture from seeping into the setting bed. Grout is available in sanded and nonsanded varieties, with or without additives.

Besides its practical function, grout plays an important design role (especially if its color contrasts with tile color) and is among the most noticeable aspects of a tile installation. Extra time and effort spent on grouting will pay off in neat, good-looking joints that will perform their duty over years of service.

Color choices have been expanded tremendously in the last few years. Your choice will depend on the color and design of your tile. If you choose a colored grout, mix a small batch and let it dry to check that the color is truly the color desired. Most packages are labeled with dye-lot numbers so you can make sure different batches are exactly the same color. Spread the test batch on an extra tile to ensure that it will not leave any traces of color on the tile fronts. If you are satisfied with the color, and the tile can be cleaned properly, proceed with grouting.

If you are tiling more than one surface in a room—the walls, floor, and countertop in a bathroom, for

instance—don't do any grouting until all surfaces are tiled and the adhesive has cured completely. Grout vertical surfaces before horizontal surfaces, countertops before floors.

Surface Preparation

As for applying thinset adhesive, the ideal temperature for grouting is from 65° to 75° F.

Be sure that the thinset adhesive has cured completely before you begin. Then, if you haven't already done so, remove spacers from grout joints. (Although some manufacturers claim their plastic spacers can be grouted over, this may cause discoloration and weakness in the grout.) Clean all excess adhesive from between tiles. (Adhesive on the tile surface should have been cleaned off during thinset application. If some remains, remove it before grouting.) Adhesive left in joints will cause problems: The joint will be weaker and the grout color may be affected. The best tools for cleaning hardened adhesive out of grout joints are a razor blade and a grout joint saw. After cleaning, vacuum dust from all tile surfaces.

Tape over any expansion joints—these will be filled with caulk later. (You should allow an expansion joint anywhere tile meets another finish surface that will not expand and contract at the same rate as the tile.) If grout does seep into expansion joints, remove it while it is still wet.

All surrounding surfaces should have been masked during earlier stages of tile installation; if they were not, mask them before grouting. When grouting nonvitreous tile, sponge or spray-mist tiles with water first. Dampen tops and edges of all tiles. Surfaces should be wet but there should be no puddles. Vitreous tile does not have to be dampened prior to grouting.

If using unglazed tile or any tile that may be stained by grout, seal the entire installation before proceeding (see page 45).

Mixing Grout

Although some grouts are available premixed, most come as separate powders that must be mixed at the job site. Use the dry-to-liquid ratios listed on the product labels. If using a color additive, mix the color into the dry ingredients before adding to the liquid. To ensure consistent color and texture, be sure to use the same measurements and mix ingredients in the same order for each batch.

Measure liquid into a mixing bucket, then add dry ingredients. Stir with a wood or plastic mixing paddle. To avoid introducing air into grout mixture, keep paddle submerged while mixing. After mixing all the ingredients, let grout rest for about 10 minutes.

Stir rested grout to remove any lumps. Consistency should be similar to cake frosting: It should hold peaks and require scooping out of mixing bucket.

Spreading Grout

Grouting, like tile setting, entails performing the same steps repeatedly, one small section at a time. The amount of time needed for each step depends on the temperature of the job site, experience of the tile setter, size of the grout joints, and size of the installation. Although the grout must set up partially during the grouting job, it is important that it does not become too hard to clean properly.

Do not attempt to grout too large an area at once because grout begins to cure as soon as it is spread. Start by grouting an area approximately three feet square. When you get a feel for the time needed to spread the grout and for it to set up partially, you can spread one section while waiting for another section to be ready for the next step. Or, if two people are working together, one can spread and one can clean and finish.

Using a grout trowel or a wide-blade squeegee, scoop enough grout out of mixing bucket to cover a small area. Don't be stingy with the grout; it is easy to scrape off the excess. Holding trowel at an angle of about 30 degrees, spread grout diagonally across tiled surface. Work grout into joints, pressing down firmly and passing over each section two or three times. Work from a different corner on each pass. Take the time to be sure that every joint is completely and evenly packed with grout. This step is the key to the success of the entire installation.

For areas too small or inaccessible to work with a trowel, use your hands. Scoop grout into the palm of your hand and spread it diagonally. Use fingers to press grout into corners.

Removing Excess

As soon as you are satisfied that all joints are completely packed, remove excess grout. Holding grout trowel at a 90-degree angle, pull it diagonally across tiled surface. Be careful to avoid creating holes in grout joints. Excess grout can be stirred back into the supply in the mixing bucket as long as it is still wet and smooth.

Once excess is removed, grout in the joints must set up partially before the section can be finished and cleaned. Set-up time varies from about 5 to 25 minutes depending on temperature and humidity.

Finishing Joints

Before the final finishing, the remaining film of grout must be removed from the surface of the tiles.

Using a sponge and many bucketfuls of clean water, clean surface of tiles. Wet the sponge but wring it out completely. Gently wipe in a circular motion. If grout in joints pulls out onto sponge, stop: Either the grout has not set up enough or the sponge is too wet. Try a drier sponge; if grout still pulls out, let it set up a bit longer. Replace water and rinse out sponge often, wringing it out after every

rinse. All excess grout should be removed after two or three passes. Avoid digging into joints as you wipe across tiles.

The grouted joints should now be smooth, even, and flush with the surface of the tile. Most importantly, all joints in an installation should be shaped in the same manner. If they are not, or if you desire slightly concave joints, make slow and gentle passes with the sponge down each joint to shave the grout down. If any areas need to be filled, push in some grout with your fingers and carefully blend it in. Rinse the sponge often (as often as every three feet) and wring it well before every pass.

Shaping joints with a margin trowel. Use a margin trowel or the handle of an old toothbrush to finish off any uneven grout joints across the field. If tile has rounded corners, round out grout joints; if tile has sharp corners, finish joints to match. Do the shaping when grout has set up but is still pliable. If grout does not hold the shape, it has not set up enough.

Once tile surfaces are free of grout and grout joints are evenly shaped, let the project rest for about 15 minutes to allow grout to continue setting up.

Final Cleanup

Make one more pass with the sponge across the installation to remove any remaining grout left on tile. The last bit of grout may not be noticeable at this point, but as it dries, a hazy film may appear on the tiles. Often this can be buffed off with a piece of clean cheesecloth. If this doesn't work, use a clean, slightly dampened sponge or piece of cheesecloth for a final wipe. Pressing firmly, make one slow, smooth pass along a row of tile. Rinse and wring out the sponge or shake out cheesecloth after each row.

It is very important to remove all traces of grout. At this stage, it is water soluble. After it dries it is not. If you discover problems after the grout has cured, there are some special cleaning products that may work. Fol-

low the manufacturer's directions carefully when using these harsh, acid-based products.

There should be no grout in expansion joints. In other joints that will be caulked, use the margin trowel to dig out enough of the grout so that, when filled, the caulked joints will be flush with the other grout joints.

Once the final cleanup is done, the grout must cure. Curing time depends on the type of grout used and is normally listed on the product label; average time is about 24 hours. Avoid walking on the tile or disturbing it until the grout has cured.

Damp Curing

Damp curing slows down the drying process, strengthening the grout bond. It is recommended for every tile installation but particularly on wet or heavily used installations. However, slow drying is not always practical, especially when you are remodeling a room that must be put back into use quickly. Whenever possible, damp cure grout on countertops around sinks, on entryway floors, and on paths and patios in freeze-thaw climates.

Damp curing merely means keeping the grout moist: Once grouting is completed, mist the entire installation with water. If practical, cover area with plastic sheeting. Keep covered for 72 hours. If you don't cover the area, mist installation with water every 24 hours for about 3 days. If you are planning to seal tiles and grout, wait about 28 days for the installation to completely cure.

Efflorescence

White haze leeching out of drying grout joints is called efflorescence. It is a natural occurrence caused by salt in the sand in adhesive and grout coming to the surface as the sand dries. It will wash away with water and eventually disappear. Wait until all traces are gone before sealing. This should take less than 28 days.

Caulking

Caulk is a waterproof, flexible seal against moisture leaking into the setting bed. Use it around bathtubs, showers, sinks, and plumbing fixtures and to fill expansion joints between walls and floors; between tubs and floors; where coved tiles meet field tiles on countertops and floors; and between wood trim and tiles. Caulk can also be used for filling small holes and cracks in walls and floors as well as for minor tile repairs.

There are two types of caulk: Those made of silicone rubber and those made of vinyl acrylic. Vinyl acrylic caulks, often called water-based caulks, can be cleaned up with water, making them a bit easier to install. Excess silicone rubber has to be scraped off. Both types are available in clear and in white as well as in a variety of colors to match colored grouts.

Apply caulk after grout has completely cured. The surface to be caulked must be clean and dry, free of any soap, oil, or grease. If grout has fallen into a joint to be caulked, remove it with a margin trowel so that the finished caulked joint will be flush with grouted joints.

Caulk is sold in tubes and cartridges; the nozzle is used as an applicator. Apply a bead of caulk to fill joint. Smooth it with your finger or with a damp sponge. Caulk seals in about 5 minutes. Any shaping and tooling should be done within that time. Depending on temperature and humidity, the joint will dry in about 24 hours; do not allow it to get wet during this period. The drying process can be speeded up with a hand-held hair dryer.

Caulking a Tub

Although it isn't discernible to the naked eye, a bathtub flexes with the weight of water and the person in it. This flexing is the major cause of cracks in caulk and grout joints.

For a superior caulk joint, fill the tub with water and get in it. This brings the tub to its lowest flex point.

Dry out joint between tub and wall with a towel and fill with caulk. (It is not quite as important that a joint be completely dry when using this type of caulk.) Tool the joint and clean up any excess material. Do not use a hand-held hair dryer on the caulk while you are in the tub. Leave water in the tub (obviously you can get out) as long as possible, up to 24 hours. By using this method, you will have filled the joint when it is most open, thereby allowing for the greatest possible flex.

Using a Caulking Gun

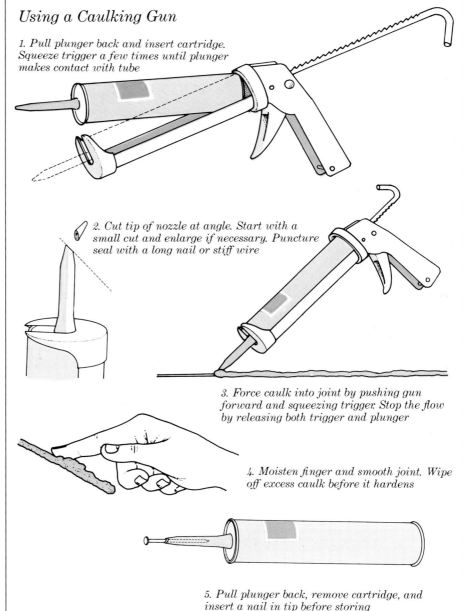

1. Pull plunger back and insert cartridge. Squeeze trigger a few times until plunger makes contact with tube

2. Cut tip of nozzle at angle. Start with a small cut and enlarge if necessary. Puncture seal with a long nail or stiff wire

3. Force caulk into joint by pushing gun forward and squeezing trigger. Stop the flow by releasing both trigger and plunger

4. Moisten finger and smooth joint. Wipe off excess caulk before it hardens

5. Pull plunger back, remove cartridge, and insert a nail in tip before storing

GLASS BLOCK

Glass has been used as an architectural element since ancient times. In the 1800s glass blocks were manufactured in metal frames and placed in pavements to admit daylight into internal spaces.

The manufacture of modern glass blocks began in the United States in 1938, and their use was embraced by architects of the Art Deco period. By the late 1970s, the popularity of glass block had waned and it was announced that the sole U.S. manufacturer would soon stop production. This announcement gave rise to a new awareness of the practical and aesthetic uses of glass block within the architectural community. Because of this, and because of the increasing use of open interiors in residential design, glass block manufacturing actually expanded.

Modern glass blocks are made by fusing two half blocks of pressed glass together; there is no frame. The vacuum produced by fusing the glass gives the block an insulation value comparable to that of insulating glass, which can help reduce energy consumption. Because of their thickness, the blocks also act as sound barriers.

When properly installed, a glass-block wall is structurally as sound as a masonry wall. This means that it can be used for security in places where pane glass could be easily broken. When an individual block does break, it implodes so that broken glass falls into the block and not out onto the floor.

Designing with Glass Block

Glass blocks have many of the attributes of glass panes, but their thickness adds another dimension. The sizes and shapes of blocks and the variety of patterns available make it possible to produce installations of great architectural interest.

Besides its aesthetic value, there are many other advantages to glass block. Used in shower and tub enclosures, it eliminates the need for any kind of protective curtain. Installed in window openings, it allows privacy without hanging shades or drapes. As a partial wall or kneewall, it divides space without separating it.

Light plays an important role in glass-block designs. Interior light shining through glass-block exterior walls at night can give a building visual appeal. Interior panels built of glass block define space and promote privacy while allowing in light. And the play of light from a flickering fire against a patterned glass-block fireplace surround is a dynamic design element. When designing walls of glass block, consider your sources of natural light and think about where you can place additional lights to take advantage of the illuminating effect of the blocks.

Although most glass blocks are made of clear or frosted glass, colored versions are available. In some cases the actual glass is colored; in others a sheet of color is added between the panels prior to fusing; and in still others the edges of the blocks are painted. Methods for adding color to an installation include using colored adhesive and grout, which will reflect color through the glass; painting the block edges yourself prior to installation; and shining colored light through the glass.

The edges of glass blocks are formed specifically to hold panel anchors, spacers, and adhesive. On an installation in which one or more edges will be exposed, you will need a finish piece to cover them. Some manufacturers offer matching end and corner pieces, and these provide the most professional-looking finish. Alternatives include filling the edge with grout and sealant or covering it with ceramic tile, perhaps to match tile used elsewhere in the building.

Buying Glass Block

Glass blocks are commonly 6, 8, or 12 inches square by 3⅛ inches thick. Half-sizes and edge and corner pieces are designed to match these basic sizes. Plan your installation so that no cutting is necessary.

The highest-quality glass blocks are designed with the pattern on the inside of the block. Those with an exterior pattern are more difficult to keep clean. Check for clarity in the glass; bubbles and irregularities are signs of a poorer-quality block. Good-quality American-made glass block carries the Underwriters' Laboratory Seal of Approval on all product boxes.

In addition to the blocks themselves, you will need panel anchors, plastic spacers, and setting materials.

Panel anchors. These are metal straps specifically designed to connect the glass blocks to the framework of an adjoining wall.

Plastic spacers. These are relatively new products manufactured specifically for use with glass blocks; they can be found wherever blocks are sold. The spacers regulate the size of the grout joints between blocks and reinforce the glass wall while the adhesive cures. Unlike tile spacers, glass-block spacers remain in place after installation.

Setting materials. Glass-block mortar mix (a white, portland-cement adhesive and additives when necessary), grout, caulk, and sealant complete the shopping list.

Glass block has become extremely popular in today's bathrooms. The installation techniques and the materials used are similar to those needed for installing tile.

Above: *Glass blocks have many virtues: They can be joined to form a structurally sound wall, they are not as transparent as glass panes, they allow light to filter through, and they are easy to clean.*

Left: *Sun shines through a glass block wall. When soaking or showering in this free-form tiled tub enclosure, the bather has a sense of privacy without feeling shut in.*

Tools for Installing Glass Block

In the past, glass block was installed by masons. Although panel anchors, plastic spacers, and modern adhesives have simplified the installation process, traditional masonry tools are still used.

To mix the glass-block adhesive, you'll need the same type of mixing tools used for thinset adhesives (see page 64). You'll also need a hammer and a screwdriver to install the anchors into a support stud.

Use a standard masonry trowel to apply adhesive, and a pointing trowel to apply the grout. You may need a raking tool to clean excess adhesive from the joints between blocks. Have a rubber mallet or a beater board handy to set the blocks into the adhesive. You'll also need a bucket of water and a sponge for cleanup, and another dry sponge for final grout-finish work.

Installing Glass Block

In order to ensure a solid, rigid glass-block wall, metal panel anchors are fastened to existing wall framing and inserted between glass blocks as the wall is built. Therefore, it is important that there be a stud where you will build the glass-block wall. If no stud exists, cut away the finish wall material and install one, toenailing it securely either to an existing stud or to both the soleplate and the top plate.

Before beginning the installation, remove any finish flooring (if installing blocks on the floor) and carefully check the site for square and level. Also make sure the area is sound and smooth. Plan the design, estimate supply needs, and have all materials and equipment on hand. Cover surrounding surfaces and mask adjoining walls and floors.

Mix adhesive according to product labels. Spread a layer of adhesive on the floor for the first row. The adhesive should not be so thick that it will be squeezed out by the weight of the block. Test the amount needed for both vertical and horizontal joints. The adhesive should fill up the channels and not ooze out along the finished edges.

Install glass blocks by building up horizontal rows. Set the first row of blocks in place one at a time, "buttering" sides with adhesive before setting blocks in place. Insert plastic spacers between blocks as you go. (On some types of spacers, there may be tabs that protrude. Don't worry about these, you'll break them off later.) Use the mallet or beater board to set blocks into adhesive. Check that all blocks are lined up horizontally and vertically and that joints are of uniform width; the success of the entire installation depends on careful placement of this first row.

When the first row is in place, spread a layer of adhesive on top of it and set the second row as you did the first. Be sure to clean adhesive from faces of blocks as you go because it is difficult to remove when dry.

The number of metal panel anchors needed depends on the size, height, and location of the installation. In general, the larger and more unsupported an installation, the more anchors are necessary to ensure rigidity. Consult salespeople for help in determining the number of anchors needed and the spacing between them. If blocks are to be installed in a window opening, attach panel anchors on both sides of the window frame.

When you have set blocks up to the height where the first anchor should be, attach anchor to a stud on the support wall, then bend it to fit into the channel on the top of the glass block.

Cover anchors and tops of all blocks in the row with adhesive, and lay the next row of blocks. Continue with subsequent rows, attaching panel anchors at appropriate intervals, until the installation is complete.

Grouting and Caulking

Allow adhesive to dry according to directions on product label (usually 24 hours), then break off exposed spacer tabs. If any adhesive has dried in the joints, clean it out with a raking tool before applying grout or caulk.

On installations that will not be exposed to water, simply grout the joints. Mix grout according to manufacturer's directions and use a pointing trowel to apply it. Using a dry sponge, push the grout into the joints so that it completely fills them. Finish joints with the sponge or your finger so they are slightly concave. Clean off excess grout before it dries.

For installations that will be exposed to water, such as the inside wall of a shower, apply silicone caulk to joints after adhesive has dried completely and before grouting.

Finishing

Apply sealant to the joints about 28 days after installing glass block; the setting materials will have cured completely by this time. Most excess adhesive, grout, and caulk should have been cleaned off already. If any remains, rub it with a piece of moistened steel wool, being careful not to scratch the glass.

Mask blocks with tape and, using a small paintbrush, apply sealant. Allow the sealant to dry before removing masking tape.

Use acid-free glass cleaner or plain water for day-to-day cleanup.

CARE & REPAIR

A lthough ease of maintenance is one of the most common reasons for choosing tile as a finish surface, this doesn't mean that tiles require no care at all. Day-to-day cleaning will ensure the beauty and longevity of your installation.

If the existing tile is in good shape but the grout joints are not or if the trim is a little out of date, you can rejuvenate rather than replace.

Tiles are susceptible to stains, damage caused by falling objects, and structural problems that can weaken or destroy the tile bond, but all of these problems can be remedied. Cracked tile, crumbled grout, and other damage can be repaired using tools you'll already have around the house, and in most cases the repairs won't take long.

Problems such as crumbling grout and a few cracked tiles can be solved without removing the entire installation.

CLEANING

T*ile is extremely easy to maintain; routine care is as simple as sweeping or vacuuming floors and regularly wiping walls and countertops with hot water and drying them with a clean cloth.*

General Maintenance

Most spills can be wiped up with a sponge or mop. For rougher scrubbing, use a stiff-bristled scrub brush or a nylon scrubbing pad. Don't use steel-wool pads on tiles; they can scratch the glaze and may cause rust stains on unglazed surfaces.

Commercial tile cleaners are available. For regular cleaning and stain removal, use products containing sodium carbonate. For deeper cleaning, use products containing caustic soda, which is 5 percent sodium hydroxide. You can make your own solution by mixing ½ cup ammonia with a gallon of water.

Read product label for specific directions and precautions before using any cleaning product. It's wise to test a new product on a spare tile or in an unobtrusive area.

Caution. Never mix cleaners that contain acid or ammonia with chlorinated bleach or with a cleaner containing bleach. Ammonia and chlorine react chemically and release a poisonous gas.

Glazed Tile

For routine care, mop or wipe glazed tiles with water and washing soda or a mild detergent. Avoid acid-based cleaners, which may eventually eat away at the glaze. Rinse well.

Periodically, you may want to restore the shine by polishing tile with a buffing machine or by hand. Waxing is generally not recommended for glazed-tile floors; wax will stick but won't penetrate, and may be transferred onto shoes and then onto surrounding carpets or wood floors.

Unglazed Tile

Unglazed tiles that have not been sealed are susceptible to staining. Fruit juices, acidic foods, and alcohol are difficult to remove from these tiles. Serving something other than spaghetti and red wine at a party on a quarry-tiled patio may be the best stain prevention. When spills do occur, prompt cleanup is advised.

For general maintenance, vacuum or sweep unglazed tile surfaces regularly to keep soil from building up in the cracks. Clean routinely with water and washing soda or a mild detergent solution. Rinse well and wipe up any standing water to prevent spotting.

Do not clean unglazed tiles with vinegar, abrasive pads, or abrasive powders. If the tiles are sealed, wax periodically with a water-based wax.

Polished Stone

Marble and other types of dimensioned stone with polished surfaces require special care. Polished stone is especially vulnerable to acids in vinegar, fruit juices, and alcohol. These can etch the surface, making it look whitish and dull.

Do not use washing soda, ammonia, or other alkaline solutions on polished stone as they will dull the finish. For best results, clean with a mild solution of soap flakes, or with a cleanser made especially for cleaning marble and similar products. Rinse well with water and let dry.

To remove stains, make a paste of soap flakes and hydrogen peroxide. Spread paste on the stain and rub in the direction of the grain. Rinse well with water and let dry. If removing the stain has etched the surface, polish with whiting (a powdered form of calcium carbonate) intended for use on polished stone.

Grout

For general grout maintenance, use a stiff brush (an old toothbrush works well) and scouring powder that does not contain bleach. Test the cleaner in a concealed area to make sure it doesn't discolor the grout. Always be on the lookout for chipped and cracked grout and repair flaws as soon as possible.

Stain Removal

To remove most stains—including ink, blood, coffee, fruit juice, wine, vegetable oil, and rust—make a thick paste of baking soda and water and apply it to the stained area. Leave on until paste is dry, then rinse with water and wipe dry. On vertical surfaces use masking tape to hold paste over stain.

Mineral deposits. Wipe with white vinegar or a solution of equal parts ammonia and water, rinse well, and pat dry. You can minimize water stains on tiled surfaces around showers, tubs, and sinks by wiping these areas dry after each use.

Mildew. Spray mildewed area with a commercial mildew remover or a chlorinated-bleach solution. Wipe with a solution of baking soda and water to remove the chlorine odor.

Stubborn stains. For stains that have penetrated deeply into the stone or bisque, use oxalic acid, which is a strong chemical bleach. Follow directions on the label carefully; it is a corrosive poison. After removing the stain, rinse tile well with water and let dry.

Oil. To remove oil from pavers (as well as from cement and bricks), use a liquid mixture of plaster of paris to draw out the stain. Brush plaster over stain, leave for 24 hours, and brush off with a broom. Repeat if necessary.

Paint. To remove paint from tile, apply a commercial paint remover, leave on for an hour, then carefully scrape off paint with a razor blade.

REJUVENATING

O ne of the major advantages of tile as a finish surface is the fact that it is very long lasting. However, this can also be a disadvantage if you don't like the look of an existing installation.

There are times when the existing tile doesn't fit in with the redecorating you want to do. Perhaps you are remodeling an older home, or maybe you are just tired of a certain look and want a change. Either way, there is no need to pull out all the tile. As long as the installation is sound, you can renovate rather than demolish.

Painting
Tile can be painted with an epoxy paint as long as the surface is carefully prepared. Although this is an inexpensive way to change tile color, epoxy paint is quite difficult to remove if you later change your mind.

Use fine-grade abrasive paper to roughen the surfaces of all tiles to be painted. Then clean the entire area thoroughly to remove all dust, dirt, and oil residue. Unless you have a steady hand and are extremely careful with brush strokes, paint grout and tile the same color. Follow instructions on paint label for application techniques and drying time.

Reglazing
Glazed tile (as well as appliances and tubs) can be reglazed to give an existing installation a completely new look. You can choose from a wide range of colors, but the tile and the grout will have to be the same color.

Reglaze only tile that is structurally sound, and have the work done by a licensed professional.

Extending a Tiled Wall
Current design trends include tiling bathtub surrounds all the way to the ceiling and tiling the entire wall area between a kitchen countertop and wall cabinets.

With a little imagination, you can extend a tiled surface even if you can't match the existing tiles. You may be able to find tiles that are very similar; if you install a row of contrasting tiles between the old and new ones, the difference will probably not be noticeable. Or you might install a checkerboard of contrasting tiles and almost-matching tiles; again, the slight variation will probably go unnoticed.

Another alternative is to dot the old installation with a few handpainted accent tiles rather than replacing an entire row.

If you plan to replace some of the existing tiles with accent tiles, or if the

Many building codes insist on fireproof surfaces around a commercial stove. Ceramic tiles will meet code, will be resistant to steam, easy to clean, and will not absorb cooking grease.

tiled area is finished with trim pieces, remove tiles using the technique described on page 90. Check that surfaces of new tiles will be flush with existing ones. Lay out and install the tile extension as you would any wall.

Extending a Tiled Floor

There's no need to replace a tiled floor when adding on to a room. If you have extra tile, simply extend the original installation.

If you cannot find a match, turn the problem into an exercise in ingenu-ity. Find a tile that matches existing ones in size and dimension and co-ordinates well with your current floor and use it to tile the addition. Then use the new tile as an accent on the old floor in a way that will tie the two floors together. This accent might take the form of a border around the edge of the existing floor or around the furnishings. You could scatter some individual tiles into the existing installation. Or, for a really strong design statement, you could lay a path of tiles leading across the exist-ing room into the addition.

Changing an Edge

New edging and trim pieces can give a countertop an updated look. The time and cost involved in changing trim are minimal compared with redoing an entire countertop, and the new look will rejuvenate a room.

Both wood trim and ceramic V-caps can replace existing square or double-bullnose edges. If you cannot find edging tiles that match the exist-ing installation, consider a contrast-ing color to add a whole new dimen-sion to your countertop.

Remove existing trim pieces using a grout knife or grout saw; see page 90. You will probably have to adjust the countertop nosing to accommo-date the new trim piece.

Adding Accent Tiles

On a tired or uninteresting installa-tion, remove tiles here and there and replace them with cheerful new ones. These bright-colored accents (or maybe they are delicately hand-painted ones) can revive the entire installation. Remove a row of tiles and replace them with a lively stripe, or replace several tiles across a field.

Be sure that new tiles are the same thickness as existing ones so that the finished installation will be smooth and level. If new tiles are thinner, build up the setting material so they will be flush with adjoining tiles.

Regrouting

Consider updating by regrouting in a color that either contrasts with or exactly matches the tile. Even if you choose to use the same color as be-fore, the new grout will give the tile installation a clean, fresh look.

Before regrouting, be sure that the installation is sound and the tile itself is in good shape. In wet installations, add a latex additive to the grout powder to help prevent cracking and crumbling. Follow regrouting direc-tions on page 91.

Current kitchen fashions include tiling the entire area between a counter and wall cabinets. This eliminates the need for trim pieces, and cut edges are obscured.

REPAIRING

Although there are many possible causes of damage, they can all be divided into two major categories: external damage and structural damage.

Isolating the Problem

Before repairing damage, you must determine the cause. This can usually be done without tearing out the tile.

External damage includes problems like chipped or broken tile, stains, missing grout, and other "surface" or cosmetic problems that have been caused by external forces—objects dropped on the tile, spills, and the like. Structural damage, on the other hand, includes cracks or unevenness across several tiles or a whole bed, and is caused by faults under the surface of the installation—leaks, a poor substrate, or a shifting foundation. External damage can usually be repaired by simply replacing the few affected tiles; structural problems are likely to require more extensive repairs.

To determine whether a problem is external or structural, first look at how many tiles are affected. If only one or two are cracked, the damage was probably caused by external forces; if cracks extend across several tiles or a whole field, the problem is probably structural. Also check whether the crack is concave (indicating a blow) or convex (indicating that the tile is being pushed out from the substrate).

If you still can't determine the cause of the damage, examine the tiles carefully: If the crack across a tile continues through the grout joint—especially in a straight line—chances are that the damage is being caused by structural forces. Press on the broken tiles; if you feel the backing

give behind them, there are problems below the surface. Smell the tiles; a musty or mildewy odor usually indicates structural damage.

If you are still unsure, recheck the crack in a few days. If it has become longer or wider since the time you first discovered it, chances are that the problem is more extensive than just a surface crack.

External Damage

If you have established that the problem does not lie underneath, you can think in terms of making cosmetic repairs.

Flaws

Tiles that have been broken, chipped, or cracked by falling objects or other external forces can simply be replaced; see opposite for instructions.

Stains

One or two badly stained tiles can ruin the look of an entire installation. These can be replaced, but before removing them, see Stain Removal on page 86.

Missing Grout

Missing grout is a common problem; grout may have dropped out or, on floors, been damaged by stiletto heels. Sometimes grout damage occurs because the adhesive was not allowed to cure long enough before grouting when the tile was installed. (Let this be a warning to you when putting in a new installation.)

The decision whether to regrout only the affected area or the whole bed is up to you. However, a grout problem in one area may be an opportunity to rejuvenate the entire installation with new grout of a different color.

Substandard Installation

A poor installation will eventually cause tile and grout to crack. Bad backing and improper application of setting materials are leading causes of tile damage.

If you don't know what substrate was put down under the tile, remove an individual tile and check that proper backing material was used. Although damage caused by poor installation is actually structural damage, you may be able to correct the situation, at least temporarily, with surface repairs. Remove and replace the broken tiles, regrout the installation, and hope for the best. Eventually, however, the entire installation will have to be replaced.

Structural Damage

Most structural damage is caused by improper installation, a less-than-solid backing, a problem in the substrate, or water damage that breaks the adhesive bond. Cracks in dimensioned stone may be an unfortunate result of a natural crack in the rock.

If tile damage is caused by structural forces, the repair will be more extensive than just the surface tile work. You must determine the exact cause and repair it as soon as possible to prevent moisture from leaking through the cracks and causing even greater problems. Some structural problems may require carpentry and plumbing repairs, which are beyond the scope of this book. You may be able to perform these repairs or you may prefer to hire a professional, but in either case you can remove and replace the tiles yourself.

Water Damage

Most structural damage is caused by water. Check the quality of the grout and caulk and make sure water and cleaning fluids are not leaking into the adhesive from the surface. Internal water damage may also be caused by dripping pipes or a leaking roof.

In the case of bad grout or caulk, remove the damaged tiles, let the installation dry completely, replace the tiles, and regrout and recaulk the installation. If the source of the water is a broken pipe, new plumbing is in order. If the problem is a leak in the building itself, you'll need to track down the location and do some carpentry work.

Settling

A shifting substrate is another common cause of cracked tile. If a floor or wall has settled, if doors and windows are difficult to open and close, and if the cracks in the tile installation seem to originate at the intersections of walls and floors, a shifting foundation is a likely culprit. If this is the case there is nothing much you can do short of jacking up the house and reinforcing or replacing the foundation.

Replacing Tiles

Before you begin tearing up tiles, be sure to mask any nearby drain holes to prevent tile pieces from clogging pipes. Cover surrounding surfaces prior to installing new adhesive, tile, and grout. Always wear safety goggles and heavy gloves when removing tiles. Tile demolition is unpredictable; pieces may fly and broken edges can be very sharp.

Replacing Single Tiles

Removing just a few tiles is a fairly simple matter, especially if you already have extra matching tiles to use as replacements. (This type of repair is one of the reasons it is a good idea to always buy extra tiles and keep the spares on hand.) If you do not have replacements and cannot match the tile, turn this hurdle into a challenge: Instead of installing a close match, replace the damaged tile with a special accent tile. You might also remove several tiles and install a pattern or a contrasting strip that will make the additions look like a renovation rather than a repair.

The tiles to be removed must first be detached from the rest of the bed so that blows do not break surrounding tiles. Clean grout from joints around the damaged tile or tiles. A hand tool called a grout knife is designed to cut through grout; a utility

knife, small hacksaw blade, or the pointed end of a church-key type of bottle opener will also do the job.

Once grout has been removed, use a hammer to break up the tile you plan to remove. Use a light touch with the hammer, delivering short, sharp blows; you should crack only the tile and not the backing. Also, the larger the pieces, the easier they will be to remove. Dig out and discard all tile pieces.

Use a putty knife, utility knife, or margin trowel to scrape off all exposed adhesive. If you do not remove all traces of adhesive, it is likely that the replacements will not seat flush with the existing tiles. Avoid using chemicals to remove the adhesive

Replacing Tile

1. Clean out grout. Break up cracked tile and remove pieces

2. Scrape off old adhesive

3. Apply new adhesive and press in new tile. Clean off excess adhesive on face of tiles and in grout joints. Hold tile in place with finishing nails or toothpicks. Wait 24 hours before grouting

residue because they can interfere with the bonding ability of the new adhesive. Remove any grout remaining around the edges and vacuum the area to get rid of all dust.

When replacing the tile, it is best to use the same adhesive as that used on the original installation. If you don't know exactly what product was used, try at least to use the same general type (either a thinset adhesive or an organic mastic).

Install the new tile by spreading a thin coat of adhesive on the back of the tile, making sure it is completely covered. Then apply more adhesive to the tile to cushion the installation. Set tile in place, use a mallet to bed it, and clean off excess adhesive. Insert finishing nails or toothpicks in the grout joints to hold tile in place. Or tape tile in place until adhesive has cured, then grout as directed on page 91.

Replacing a Field of Tiles

If you are replacing an entire field of tiles for purely aesthetic reasons, and not to correct a structural problem, remember that you can install new tile over existing tile (see page 38).

If you are removing all the tile from a countertop, you will find it much easier to remove and replace the entire top than to remove the grout, break and remove the tiles individually, and then scrape away all adhesive from the backing.

If you are removing tile installed on wallboard or CBU (Cementitious Backer Units), you can remove tiles individually, as described above, or pull out the entire backing and replace it, as described below. You will probably find that spending the minimal amount of money required for a new piece of wallboard or CBU is preferable to scraping the adhesive off an entire installation.

Use a utility knife or a saw to cut through the wallboard around the tile installation. You may need to scrape away grout or caulk around the outside edge of the field in order to see the backing. Take care to cut through the wallboard only and not through any wiring or plumbing behind the wall. (Shut off power first.) Use a pry bar or the claw end of a hammer to pull wallboard away from studs. If the wall does not come loose, make additional cuts toward the center of the installation. Try not to put a lot of strain on the surrounding wall as you work the panel away from the studs. It should come away in fairly large pieces, so enlist some help. Pull nails out of studs before installing a new substrate.

Tile set on plywood. You can remove a field of tiles individually from a plywood backing, scrape away the adhesive, and retile. However, the cost of a new piece of plywood is low enough that you'll probably want to simply remove and replace the plywood. If you choose to retain a plywood backing, be sure to remove all old adhesive and clean the plywood before installing new tile.

To remove tiles and plywood backing together, use a Carborundum® blade to saw through both layers. Be sure to cut through only the tile and plywood and not into wiring and plumbing; play it safe and shut off power before cutting. Cut around the perimeter of the field, then make enough vertical and horizontal cuts within the field to divide it into manageable pieces. Pry out these pieces and discard them.

Pull any remaining nails before installing a new substrate.

Tile set in mortar or concrete. Removing a field of tiles set in a traditional mortar bed or on a concrete slab is a back-breaking task. Remember that if your plan is to install new tiles, they can be set over the existing installation (see page 38).

Tile can be removed from a mortar floor, wall, or countertop in two ways. Neither method allows for reusing the setting bed; this must be removed as well. One method is to break up tiles with a hammer, remove broken tiles,

cut up the reinforcing mesh with wire cutters, and then remove the setting bed using a pry bar. The other is to make several cuts through both the tile and the mortar using a saw fitted with a Carborundum® blade. Then insert a pry bar into the cuts and pull the installation away in chunks.

To remove tile from a concrete slab, use a hammer to break the tile, then pry off pieces and scrape away the remaining setting materials. Be sure the field is free of all tile chips and dust prior to installing new tile.

Grout Problems

Cracked or crumbling grout may be the first indication of a structural problem or it may simply be due to a bad grouting job or wear and tear.

In installations that are exposed to water, grout problems may be caused by leaks behind the tile that are forcing the grout out. First check that joints around plumbing fixtures are properly caulked; these are the most likely sources of leaks. If they do not seem to be leaking, simply regrout cracked joints. If the caulk looks stained, dry, or brittle, pull it out and let the area dry completely (you might help this along with a hand-held hair dryer), then recaulk.

In dry installations, cracks in grout may be due to a shifting substrate. Some shifting is common in a new house, as is some seasonal settling in older construction. Before tearing out the entire tile installation, try regrouting cracked joints. If the cracks recur, the problem may be the adhesive, the backing, the substrate, or the foundation, and you should check the directions for tile repair discussed above.

Regrouting

If cracks in the grout are fairly small and clean, leave existing grout in place and simply apply new grout over it. If cracks are large or dirty, or if you are regrouting the tile installation for renovation purposes, the ex-

isting grout must be removed before regrouting.

Remove grout using a grout saw, which is specifically designed for this purpose. A utility knife, the pointed edge of a church-key type of bottle opener, the edge of a trowel, or a small hacksaw blade will also do the trick. Once most of the grout is out of the joints, vacuum away any dust. Clean tiles to remove all dirt, oil, and soap scum before grouting.

Unless you are regrouting the entire installation, be sure that new grout matches the original in color. Borrow grout color samples from a tile store to find the closest shade. A slight variance in color will probably go unnoticed, but if color match is very important, mix up a small batch of grout, let it dry for three or four days, and check color before making a final decision.

Replacing Grout

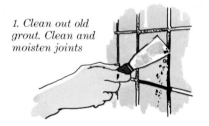

1. Clean out old grout. Clean and moisten joints

2. Apply new grout. Smooth and clean off excess

TILE TERMINOLOGY

T *he following are terms used in the tile industry and throughout this book.*

Apron: Trim or facing on the side or front of a countertop, table edge, or windowsill.

Back-butter: The method of applying adhesive to the back of a tile to supplement the adhesive on the setting bed. Used for trim tiles and small tiles and with any tile with an uneven back to ensure a strong bond.

Bed or deck: The surface to be tiled.

Bisque: The mixture of clay, water, and additives that is shaped into the body of a tile.

Blanks: Tiles that can be painted. These can be found in many craft-supply stores.

Body: Structural portion of a ceramic product and the material or mixture from which it is made.

Bond: The resistance from separation between tile and adhesive.

Broken joint: Ceramic-tile installation featuring each row off-set for half its length.

Bullnose: A trim tile with a convex radius on one side. Used for finishing the top of a wainscot or turning an outside corner.

Button-back tile: Tile manufactured with raised dots on back, which separate the individual tiles when they are stacked in the kiln.

Caulk: A soft, flexible waterproof material used to seal seams around sinks and plumbing fixtures and to finish expansion joints.

Cement-bodied tile: Whereas ceramic tile is made of clay, this tile is made of mortar. It has the appearance of stone or paver tile, is quite durable, and is less expensive than its ceramic counterpart.

Cement mortar: A mixture of sand, cement, and water used for preparing traditional tile-setting beds.

Cementitious backer unit (CBU): A manufactured panel of cement and fiberglass mesh, $1/4$ inch, $7/16$ inch, or $1/2$ inch thick, used as an underlayment for the installations.

Chlorinated polyethylene (CPE) membrane: A waterproofing covering sold in sheet form, which is applied to setting beds.

Cove: A trim tile with one edge formed as a concave radius. Used to form a junction between the bottom wall course and the floor.

CTI: The Ceramic Tile Institute, established in 1954, tests new products related to the tile industry.

Cure: The time that a tile installation must be left alone and allowed to set for it to reach full strength.

Damp curing: The process of slowing down the curing process by keeping grout moist for 2 to 3 days. This strengthens the grout bond.

Deck or bed: The surface to be tiled.

Decorative tile: Any tile face decorated by hand-painting or affixed with decals prior to firing.

Dimensioned stone or gauged stone: Rough-hewn or polished stone cut to an even thickness and dimension.

Down angle: A trim tile with two rounded or curved edges that is used to finish off outside corners.

Expansion joint or perimeter joint: The intentional interruption of a field of tile to allow for seasonal movement in the setting bed. Filled with caulk for flexibility.

Faience tile: Tile with variations in the face, edges, and glaze that give a hand-crafted, non-mechanical, decorative effect.

Feature strip: A narrow strip of tile with contrasting color, texture, or design.

Field: The main area of a tile installation.

Firing: Controlled heat treatment in a kiln or furnace to develop desired properties in ceramic tile.

Floated bed: A cement mortar installation.

Floating: Spreading and smoothing mortar with a tool called a float.

Floor tile: A ceramic, glazed or unglazed paver, quarry, or mosaic tile resistant to abrasion and impact.

Gauged stone: See dimensioned stone.

Glazed tile: An impermeable, smooth-surfaced tile with a colored, opaque glaze fused to the face during firing. The glaze may be high-gloss, semi-matte, or matte with a smooth or textured surface.

Grout: Sand-and-cement based material for filling joints between tiles, available in a variety of colors, some with easy-to-clean and mildew-resistant features. Epoxy-based grouts are stain resistant and ideal for kitchen floors.

Grout joints: The space between tiles that is filled with grout.

Impervious tile: Dense-bodied tile fired at extremely high temperature for a long period of time.

Inside corner: Trim tile made specifically for turning a right angle inside a wall corner.

Jury stick or story pole: A measuring device created for a particular tile installation. Units of measure indicate the width of the tiles and the grout joints between. It helps determine how many tiles will be needed for a given area and can be used when positioning layout lines.

Latex or acrylic thinset adhesive: One of three types of sand-and-cement-based thinset tile adhesives.

Layout lines or reference lines: Guidelines chalked on a setting bed used to accurately position tile.

Level: When all points are at the same elevation and are horizontally straight.

Lugs: Protrusions on tiles designed to maintain even spacing for grout joints.

Mastic: Tile adhesives made from organic substances.

Mosaic tile: Square, round, or octagonal tiles that are usually $1/4$ inch to $3/8$ inch thick with a facial area of less than 4 square inches.

Mounted tile: Tile assembled into units or sheets, either back mounted or face mounted, and bonded to facilitate handling. Also called panels.

Mud: Slang term for cement mortar.

Natural clay tile: A ceramic mosaic or paver tile made by the dust-pressed method. Made from clays that produce a dense body with a slightly textured appearance.

Nonvitreous tile: A soft-bodied porous tile that is fired at a lower temperature and for a shorter period of time than impervious tile. Nonvitreous tile is very absorbent and not freeze-thaw stable.

Organic mastic: A petroleum- or latex-based setting material manufactured ready-to-use. It has less bond and comprehensive strength and is more easily damaged by water and is less flexible than thinset adhesives.

Outside corner: Trim tile made specifically for wrapping around the corner of two intersecting surfaces.

Panels: Another term for groups of tile mounted on mesh sheets.

Paver tile: Unglazed porcelain, natural clay, or shale tile formed by the dust-pressed method. Usually thicker than a floor tile. Generally 12 inches square or star-shaped. Popular in Mediterranean designs and often referred to as Mexican tiles.

Perimeter joint or expansion joint: The joint found at the intersection of interior floors and walls that allows for seasonal expansion in the floor or wall.

Plumb: A line perpendicular to a level surface.

Pregrouted tile: An assembly of ceramic tile, bonded at the edges by material (generally elastomeric) that completely seals the joints.

Reference lines or layout lines: Guidelines chalked on a setting bed used to accurately position tile.

Retarder additive: An ingredient added to adhesive and grout that slows down the evaporation of liquid from the setting material, slowing down the curing time and strengthening the bond.

Sculptured tile: Tile with a decorative design of high and low relief molded into the face.

Sealer: Protective coating applied to the surface of unglazed tile.

Self-spacing tile: Tile with lugs, spacers, or other protrusions that create grout joints between the tiles.

Semi-vitreous tile: A somewhat porous tile fired longer than nonvitreous tile. This tile absorbs moisture and is not freeze-thaw stable.

Setting bed: The surface where the tile is set.

Set-up time: How long it takes adhesive spread on a surface to begin curing or hardening.

Slip-resistant tile: Tile having greater slip resistance due to the addition of an abrasive component in the tile mixture, abrasive particles in the surface, or grooves or patterns in the surface.

Story pole: See jury stick.

Substrate: Backing material used under a tile installation.

Substrate sealer: A liquid waterproofing membrane applied to the substrate.

TCA: The Tile Council of America was established in 1945 and is made up of companies producing tile and related products. This organization sets installation specifications and promotes the industry.

Thick-bed installation: Traditional tile-installation method using cement mortar.

Thick-bed mortar: A thick layer of cement mortar (more than ½ inch) that is used for leveling.

Thin-bed or thinset installation: A method of bonding tile with setting materials not greater than ¼ inch in thickness.

Thinset adhesive: Water-mixed, latex, and epoxy thinset are three types of setting materials that must be mixed with a liquid. Compared to organic adhesives, thinset produces a greater bond and comprehensive strength, sets up more quickly, is more flexible when dry, and is more heat and water-resistant.

Tile nippers: Special pliers that nibble away little bites of ceramic tile. Used to create or clean out small, irregular, or curved cuts.

Tile spacer: Plastic device placed between tiles to create a uniform grout joint.

Trim tile: Tile glazed on one or more edges and produced in various shapes to edge counters, turn corners, or provide a finished edge to a tile installation.

Unglazed tile: Fire-hardened clay tiles with color that runs throughout the tile.

Up angle: Trim tile designed with a curved corner used to finish an inside corner.

V-cap: Trim tile used on the front edge of a countertop.

Vitreous tile: Dense, nonporous tile that is fired at a higher temperature for a longer period of time than nonvitreous tile. It absorbs very little moisture, has a high comprehensive strength, and is freeze-thaw stable.

Waterproofing membrane: Usually a chlorinated polyethylene (CPE) membrane placed on the setting bed, under the tile, to protect the substrate from damage by water.

METRIC CHART

U.S. Measure and Metric Measure Conversion Chart

	Formulas for Exact Measures				*Rounded Measures for Quick Reference*		
	Symbol	*When you know:*	*Multiply by:*	*To find:*			
Mass (Weight)	oz	ounces	28.35	grams	1 oz		= 30 g
	lb	pounds	0.45	kilograms	4 oz		= 115 g
	g	grams	0.035	ounces	8 oz		= 225 g
	kg	kilograms	2.2	pounds	16 oz	= 1 lb	= 450 g
					32 oz	= 2 lb	= 900 g
					36 oz	= 2¼ lb	= 1000 g (1 kg)
Volume	tsp	teaspoons	5.0	milliliters	¼ tsp	= 1/24 oz	= 1 ml
	tbsp	tablespoons	15.0	milliliters	½ tsp	= 1/12 oz	= 2 ml
	fl oz	fluid ounces	29.57	milliliters	1 tsp	= 1/6 oz	= 5 ml
	c	cups	0.24	liters	1 tbsp	= ½ oz	= 15 ml
	pt	pints	0.47	liters	1 c	= 8 oz	= 250 ml
	qt	quarts	0.95	liters	2 c (1 pt)	= 16 oz	= 500 ml
	gal	gallons	3.785	liters	4 c (1 qt)	= 32 oz	= 1 liter
	ml	milliliters	0.034	fluid ounces	4 qt (1 gal)	= 128 oz	= 3¾ liter
Length	in.	inches	2.54	centimeters	⅜ in.	= 1 cm	
	ft	feet	30.48	centimeters	1 in.	= 2.5 cm	
	yd	yards	0.9144	meters	2 in.	= 5 cm	
	mi	miles	1.609	kilometers	2½ in.	= 6.5 cm	
	km	kilometers	0.621	miles	12 in. (1 ft)	= 30 cm	
	m	meters	1.094	yards	1 yd	= 90 cm	
	cm	centimeters	0.39	inches	100 ft	= 30 m	
					1 mi	= 1.6 km	
Temperature	°F	Fahrenheit	5/9 (after subtracting 32)	Celsius	32° F	= 0° C	
					68°F	= 20°C	
	°C	Celsius	9/5 (then add 32)	Fahrenheit	212° F	= 100° C	
Area	in.^{2}	square inches	6.452	square centimeters	1 in.^{2}	= 6.5 cm^2	
	ft^2	square feet	929.0	square centimeters	1 ft^2	= 930 cm^2	
	yd^2	square yards	8361.0	square centimeters	1 yd^2	= 8360 cm^2	
	a.	acres	0.4047	hectares	1 a.	= 4050 m^2	

INDEX